Mothuſye flu
Llauern flu
Hill
Bowſe Wood
Auon vaue
Narnia
Kemmer Abbey
olgelhe
MOWT HY
Dovye flu
HUND.

THE BOOK OF HARLECH

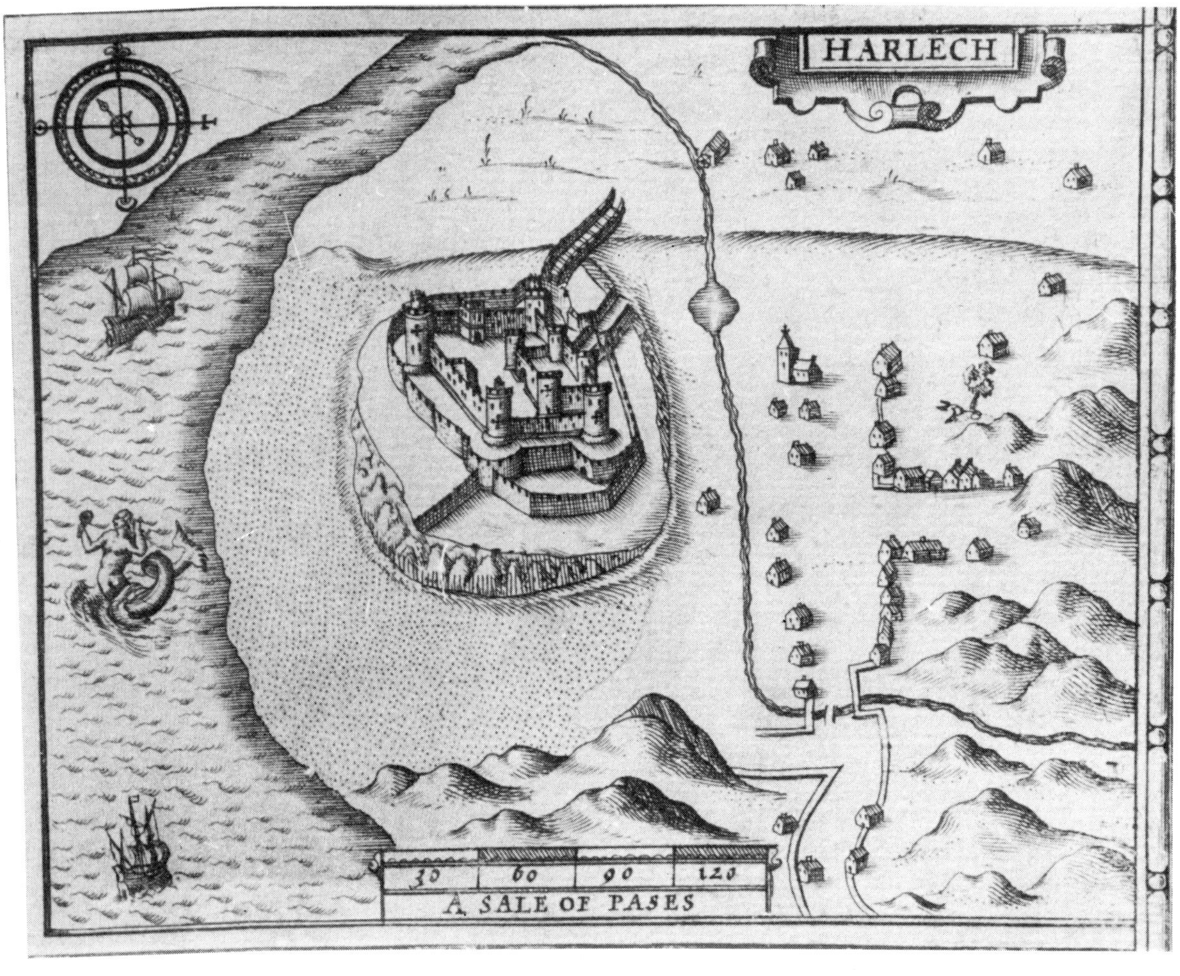

FRONT COVER: The Harlech inset to John Speede's map of Merioneth, 1610. (CH)

'Beti Ffransis' (1812-1896), Mrs Richards of Iwerddon, Harlech, butter merchant. Stocking knitting was virtually a leisure activity in Merioneth. (BEE)

THE BOOK OF HARLECH

Time-touched Stone

BY

LEWIS WILLIAM LLOYD

LLB (Wales), LLM (Cantab), PhD (ANU), FSA

BARRACUDA BOOKS LIMITED
BUCKINGHAM, ENGLAND
MCMLXXXVI

BARRACUDA BOOKS LIMITED
BUCKINGHAM, ENGLAND
MCMLXXXVI

PUBLISHED BY BARRACUDA BOOKS LIMITED
BUCKINGHAM, ENGLAND
AND PRINTED BY
EBENEZER BAYLIS & SON LIMITED,
WORCESTER, ENGLAND.

BOUND BY
HUNTER & FOULIS LTD,
EDINBURGH, SCOTLAND

JACKET PRINTED BY
CHENEY & SONS LIMITED
BANBURY, OXON

PHOTOLITHOGRAPHY BY
SOUTH MIDLANDS LITHOPLATES LIMITED
LUTON, ENGLAND

DISPLAY SET IN BASKERVILLE
AND TEXT SET IN 10½/12pt BASKERVILLE BY
KEY COMPOSITION
NORTHAMPTON, ENGLAND

ISBN 0 86023 280 8

Contents

Acknowledgements

This book is the result of numerous conversations and discussions with many Harlech and Ardudwy people over the past 30 years or so and consequently, several of them are no longer alive. I am most grateful to them all but must mention my especial gratitude to the late Mr Richard Edwards of Gorffwysfa, Harlech, and to his daughter, the late Mrs Beti Ellis Evans. I am also particularly indebted to my father, the late Mr Lewis Pugh Lloyd of Y Berth, Llanfair, to his eldest sister, the late Mrs Mary Pugh Humphreys of 7 Rock Terrace, Harlech, and to her elder son, my cousin, Mr Gwilym Lloyd Humphreys of Bryn-Môr, Llanfair. It would be impossible to mention every one by name so I can merely say thank you to them all.

I am also greatly indebted to the Librarian and staff of the National Library of Wales, Aberystwyth; Ann Rhydderch MA DAA, the Meirionnydd Archivist, Dolgellau, and her staff and Bryn Parry MA DAA, the Gwynedd County Archivist, and his staff at Caernarfon for their cheerfulness and unstinted helpfulness during more years than they or I would care to remember, in relation to this as to so many other projects. They have ensured that the Gwynedd Archives Service has no superior throughout Britain.

Institutions and individuals are acknowledged elsewhere for the provision of illustrations, but here I must mention my friend and collaborator of many years standing, Mr Martin Eckley BA ALA, the Librarian of Coleg Harlech, the instigator and publisher of *Hen Dref Harlech a Phentre Llanfair* (1981) and *Cwmwd Ardudwy* (1984); Mrs Valmai Owen and Mrs Mena Ifans of Coleg Harlech for their assistance and encouragement at crucial times in the preparation of this book; Mr Michael Watts BA for his photographic work provided generously in his spare time, and Mr Anton Bantock for allowing me to copy the unpublished memoirs of his kinswoman, Mrs Constance Lyne, for deposit in the Record Office at Dolgellau. To all others who have assisted in this study of Harlech I can but say: Diolch yn fawr i chi gyd (Thanks very much to you all).

Every effort has been made to verify the details recorded and to support the opinions expressed, but any errors of fact or judgement that remain are my sole responsibility.

Finally, I must thank all those who have assisted in gaining subscriptions for the limited edition of this book — Jim and Betty Yuill of Castle Cottage, Augusto Gatta of the Castle Hotel and many others — and express my gratitude to Mr Clive Birch on behalf of the publishers, which is heartfelt, for the patience and tact shown to this somewhat wayward author.

Key to Caption Credits

AB	Mr Anton Bantock
AW	Mrs Arlene Wofford
BEE	Mrs Beti Ellis Evans
CH	Coleg Harlech
EW	Mrs Eifiona Williams
GAP	Mr Gwilym Artro Pugh
GAS	Gwynedd Archives Service
JH	Miss Jane Humphreys
JN	Mr James Nelson
JW	Miss Jane Williams
MPH	Mrs Mary Pugh Humphreys
MR	Megan Reeves
MU	Mary Unwin
MW	Michael Watts
NLW	National Library of Wales
UCNWA	University College of North Wales Archives
USNA	United States National Archives
WJW	Mr William J. Williams

Foreword

by Jim Yuill, Chairman, Harlech and District Tourism Association

The town of Harlech has long been one of those places where the chance visitor is surprised and delighted by the richness of its history, the charm of its location and the hospitality of its people. For this reason it deserves to be more widely known and appreciated, and all of us who are fortunate enough to reside there are grateful to the author and publishers of this book for bringing this about. Having read this book, those who know the town and the surrounding district will have enriched their knowledge, and those who do not know it will surely be tempted to come and see for themselves.

Castle Cottage,
Harlech

Jim Yuill

Dedication

For my mother and in memory of my father.

Gwŷr Harlech

As this book is in English it seems appropriate here to set down the stirring Welsh words of John Ceiriog Hughes, written in about 1860, for the already famous *March of the Men of Harlech (Rhyfelgyrch Gwŷr Harlech)*. The music was first published in 1784, though the march or 'war song' was inspired by the defence of Harlech Castle by Dafydd ab Ieuan ab Einion and his companions in the 15th century.

(1) Wele goelcerth wen yn fflamio,
A thafodau tân yn bloeddio
Ar i'r dewrion ddod i daro
Unwaith eto'n un;
Gan fanllefau'r tywysogion,
Llais gelynion, trwst arfogion,
A charlamiad y marchogion,
Craig ar graig a grŷn!
Cwympa llawer llywydd,
Arfon byth ni orfydd:
Cyrff y gelyn wrth y cant
Orffwysant yn y ffosydd:
Yng ngoleuni'r goelcerth acw,
Tros wefusau Cymro'n marw
Annibyniaeth sydd yn galw
Am ei dewraf dyn!

(2) Ni chaiff gelyn ladd ac ymlid;
Harlech! Harlech! cwyd i'w herlid!
Y mae Rhoddwr mawr ein rhyddid
Yn rhoi nerth i ni;
Wele Gymru a'i byddinoedd
Yn ymdywallt o'r mynyddoedd!
Rhuthrant fel rhaeadrau defroedd,
Llamant fel y lli!
Llwyddiant i'n lluyddion
I rwystro bâr yr estron;
Gwybod yn ei galon gaiff
Fel bratha cleddyf Brython!
Cledd yn erbyn cledd a chwery,
Dur yn erbyn dur a dery;
Wele faner Gwalia i fyny,
Rhyddid aiff a hi.

To these martial lines may be added A. G. Bradley's reflections in his *In Praise of North Wales* (1925):

When I first set eyes on the little townlet in the mid-eighties, stretching along the high ridge beside its overawing castle, it catered, I think, very little for visitors. I well remember, as I looked down upon the furzy sheep pasture stretching to the sand hills half a mile away, which shut out the sea, saying to a companion who understood, 'What a golf-course this would make!' There was not one in all Wales at that time and barely a dozen in all England. Ten years later I was playing over the beginnings of the beautiful course that now exists, and is known throughout the golfing world. It has crowded Harlech in the holiday season with visitors, occasioned the building of a great hotel and quite a string of private residences . . . Winter, too, deals tenderly with Harlech, while the east winds of early spring rage impotently against the back of the mountain wall beneath whose front it shelters. And again, the sunsets of that season, as seen from here over Cardigan Bay on a calm sea, are unforgettable. That glittering band of gold which from the horizon, in every-broadening trail, spreads its radiant effulgence, to fade only on the very sand dunes at our feet. For one is always high up at Harlech, looking over a wide sea and an amazingly varied world of mountain and plain.

Introduction

Why should time and effort be expended upon the history of so small a town as Harlech? In the period immediately following the construction of the Castle it is unlikely that the population, the regular garrison and the people of the borough, exceeded 100 and even in the last century the inhabitants numbered under 500. The present population is about three times the latter figure for the greater part of each year. How then can this study be justified? Apart from the fact that it is the first of its kind in English (or Welsh), the primary justification is that the history of Harlech is not merely long but eventful. In spite of its apparent remoteness, Harlech has been touched and troubled at several points by general historical developments and has been the scene of more stirring martial episodes than have many much larger communities. It certainly possesses a unique place in Welsh history. For this we may thank or curse the fortress of Edward I, the successor of earlier Welsh fortifications raised either on or near the same site. This may well be conceded, but my second justification is rather more difficult to sustain. When the Castle lost its military significance (this occurred at no precise point, though it was beyond doubt by 1650) Harlech became, in effect, a village community whose collective memories of more dramatic times were sustained by a mouldering yet still impressive ruin, and by the tenuous survival of borough and county town status into the 19th century. Of what possible interest can Harlech's long decline in significance be to anyone not intimately acquainted with the town and district by residence or family ties or both? Yet, fairly close study of a small community and its matrix can be of interest to outsiders, provided it is not myopic, but one which seeks to derive general sense and meaning from local events and developments. The vicissitudes of Welsh rural life during the past two centuries or so need not be matters of purely local concern.

The past certainly inhabits the present at Harlech, for the Castle refuses to be ignored (not least with regard to television reception) even though, for most of the inhabitants, it is almost part of the natural scenery, like the rock upon which it stands. Some Welsh people, including this writer, feel uneasy within the Castle. I feel like an intruder, and is it mere fancy on my part to detect an air of bold assurance in the bearing of many English visitors as they enter the Castle and walk around its battlements?

In writing this account I have been conscious throughout of my Welshness, and descent from the working people of Ardudwy who almost literally bore the privileged upon their backs. A crowd of silent witnesses stood by as I wrote, and I hope, at times, to have spoken for them, as they were unable to express themselves in life. Objectivity is impossible but fairness may be, perhaps, a realistic objective.

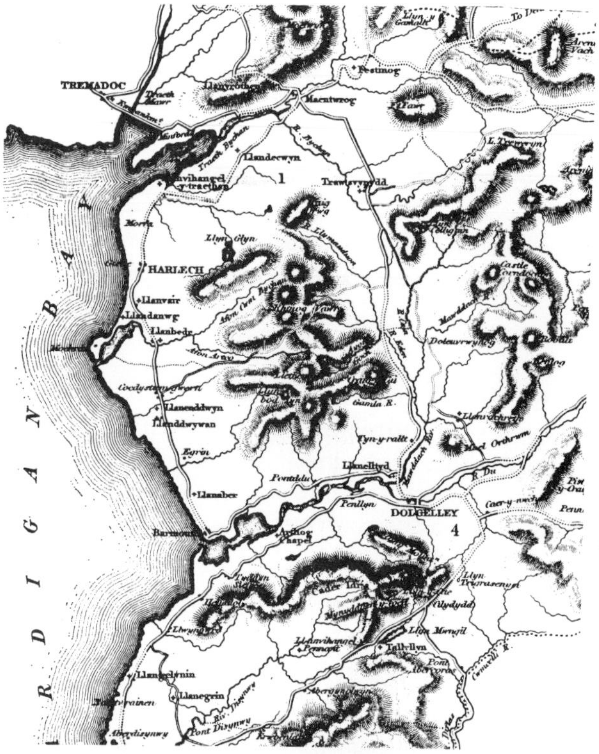

LEFT: A southern prospect from the former Castle green. RIGHT: Ardudwy and South Merioneth from a map of the county of 1842. BELOW: The town and castle from the air by Aerofilms Ltd. (All GAS)

Harlech in Ardudwy

The town of Harlech, dominated by its late 13th century Castle, is situated on a craggy and abrupt westward-facing slope close to the shoreline of Cardigan Bay. It lies in the ancient parish of Llandanwg, within the Diocese of Bangor, one of thirteen parishes which, with Nanmor in Beddgelert parish, constituted the Welsh *cwmwd* and the post-conquest hundred of Ardudwy. Below the castle rock and northwards extend the flat, sandy, wastes of *Morfa Harlech* which were called, in mediaeval times, the 'Harlech Marsh or 'Great Marsh'. Once noted for its horses, the Morfa (lit. sea-place) provides good grazing for cattle and sheep and an abundant crop of hay more often than not. It has been put to several other uses in the modern era.

The rest of Llandanwg parish is composed largely of upland pastures and sheepwalks, punctuated by scattered sturdy farmhouses and divided by an irregular mesh of stone walls, the more or less enduring symbols of early 19th century enclosures. Some of these walls are, however, the remains of *buarthau*, cattle folds, which serve as a reminder that the rearing of and trade in cattle have been the mainstay of the local economy since unremembered times. Sheep came later and, with them in the middle ages, knitting and weaving were added to the manufacture of leather and leather goods as the main local crafts. Horses and goats were reared also on these windswept and rain-lashed acres. These uplands (*ffriddoedd*) provide impressive vantage points since they command fine views of *Eryri* ('Snowdonia'), the estuaries of the rivers Dwyryd and Glaslyn to the north, and of the river Mawddach to the south, beyond the austere yet rounded forms of the Rhinog mountains, the weathered stumps of a once mighty mountain range. Though peopled more or less continuously for thousands of years, as the maenhirs (standing stones), cromlechs (chambered tombs), Iron Age hill forts and other ancient sites attest, this rugged hinterland remains a mysterious country beyond the sound of the sea; no one can ever fully penetrate its mystery and, perhaps, no one should ever try. Harlech lies between these untamed uplands and the coastal plain, and is bound to the rock as firmly as the Castle which has made its name famous throughout the world. The Castle dominates the town and presides over its immediate surroundings to cast a long shadow over the quick and the dead.

This corrugated pastoral district of *Ardudwy* — the name may be Irish in origin — contains deposits of lead, copper, gold, manganese, slate and other minerals which were exploited notably during the 19th century. In fact, until the present century, all the main occupations of the district can be said to have been elemental in character: pastoral farming, mining, quarrying, fishing and seafaring. The historian can but try to provide a faithful account of human settlement and activity manifested in ancient sites, in stone structures and in the spaces cleared between rocks, small and transient 'conquests' painfully achieved from thin and acid soils and recorded in the mountainous spoil of the district's once great and one great industry, the production of fine roofing slates, which were carried all over the world in vessels commanded and commonly manned by men of the district. Over the centuries, the people of Harlech have been drawn principally from these rock-strewn uplands and they knew too well the unending struggle for survival and the bitterness of defeat, defeat which mocks the presumption of Edward I as a 'conqueror'.

The Romans seem to have been content to contain the district and its defenders by means of small forts at *Tomen-y-Mur* in Trawsfynydd parish and at Brithdir near Dolgellau, but they left various elements of their civilisation. The sea which brought waves of settlers and invaders to Ardudwy from prehistoric times also carried Christian missionaries of the Celtic Church ('saints') to these shores in the 5th and 6th centuries. Most of the early religious foundations were located near the seashore or within reach of the sea, by boat, on river banks. Ardudwy provides ample evidence of this coastwise movement. The 'saints' seem to have included Tanwg (Llandanwg — *llan* signifies a religous enclosure) and Enddwyn (Llanenddwyn), and other religious sites were dedicated to holy men for whom there are dedications in many other parts of Wales (*eg:* Illtyd as in Llanelltyd on the river Mawddach).

The conventional view is that Wales (*Cymru*) was weakened during the 'Age of the Princes' by internecine conflicts between the many territorial rulers. Such conflicts certainly diverted attention from the growing threat posed by the Saxons and then by the Normans but, like the Saxons under Harold, the Welsh were conquered eventually when they were quite effectively united under a 'Prince of Wales', Llywelyn ap Gruffydd, grandson of Llywelyn the Great, whose title was confirmed by Henry III and Edward I of England. The death of a widely acknowledged leader can be decisive in a struggle against alien domination — it was clearly so in England in 1066 and in Wales in 1282. Unity can be a source of weakness as well as of strength.

Legends suggest that the castle site had been fortified in much earlier times. No physical remains have been found, but the builders of the Castle, as servants of Edward I, may have been instructed to efface the sites and memories of a defeated people. Yet folk memories survived and, for this writer, as for many others, the grim fortress of Edward I is haunted by the shades of Bendigaid Fran and his fair sister Branwen (or Bronwen), Maelgwn Gwynedd and Collwyn ap Tangno (hence the name *Caercollwyn*) and not merely by the spectres of those for whom history has a more substantial record. The castle rock was too good a defensive site to be ignored by earlier generations, who had much to fear from what the sea might carry hither.

Finally, the name 'Harlech' demands brief consideration. Most students of Welsh place-names now seem confident that 'Harlech' is derived from *Hardd-(1)lech* which signifies a beautiful slope, an apt description. One scholar, Sir John Rhys, suggested a possible Scandinavian origin, but he seems to have been misled by mediaeval renderings. These included 'Hardelawe', 'Hardelewe', 'Hardlagh', 'Hardelagh', and 'Hardleigh', but such renderings are unreliable. It is not uncommon for several versions to appear in the same document. *Harddlech*, the *llys* (court) of Bendigaid Fran in the *Mabinogi* (or *Mabinogion* — a cycle of ancient stories) is a more convincing original and, by the 18th century, the form *Hardlech* is quite commonly encountered. The latter form is readily pronounced 'Harlech', though, locally, the name is usually pronounced 'Harl*a*ch'.

ABOVE: The Castle and town from the west by Aerofilms Ltd. The woodland to the north (left) was donated to the National Trust by A. P. Graves, Erinfa. LEFT: The Castle and its eastern backdrop by Aerofilms Ltd. RIGHT: Part of Morfa Harlech and Tremadog Bay from the air to the east of Harlech by Aerofilms Ltd. (All GAS)

LEFT: The Castle's imposing keep-like Gate House and the former mill pond (*Llyn-y-Felin*). RIGHT: The Gate House's graceful façade from the Inner Ward. (Both GAS) BELOW: The town's ancient corn mill as engraved by Walker and Angus after Paul Sandby, 1779. (NLW)

Garrison Town

The death of Llywelyn ap Gruffydd, the last native Prince of Wales, near Builth in December 1282, dealt a savage blow to Welsh aspirations. What the common people felt at this time will never be known, but the bards raised a powerful lamentation. In the following year, Edward I proceeded to effect the conquest of Gwynedd, the bastion of Welsh resistance. He advanced to Conwy in March 1283 and sent an army under Otto de Grandison and John de Vescy along the coast from Caernarfon to Harlech. Communications were maintained by sea. A ring of massive stone fortresses was then planned to keep the Welsh in awe of their alien rulers; plans were also laid to create boroughs and to people them with Anglo-Norman settlers as centres of colonial rule. The process had long been familiar elsewhere (not least in England) and many other subject peoples were to experience similar methods in the future: England's imperial teeth were cut on Wales (the conquest of Ireland was more of a free-booting exercise, launched from south Wales, than a concerted imperial design). Wales (the 'Principality' beyond the 'Marches') became a 'dominion' or colony until Wales (including parts of the Marches) was virtually annexed to England during the reign of Henry VIII. Llywelyn ap Gruffydd's wooden hall at Ystumgwern, Dyffryn Ardudwy, was soon to be transported some five miles to Harlech and installed in the Castle as a symbol of the new order.

Some preliminary work was commenced at Harlech in 1283 (principally the rock-cut ditch on the eastern or town side of the future fortress) and the first Constable, Hugh de Longslow, was appointed in October 1284 at an annual salary of £100, out of which he was to maintain a garrison of 30 men. The garrison was to include 10 crossbowmen, a chaplain, an *artiller* (*artilliator* — a maker of arrows, lances and other weapons), a smith, a carpenter and a mason, while others were to be janitors, watchmen and other necessary ministers ('et alii Ministri qui necessarii sunt in Castro'). By Charter of Edward I in 1284 (Welsh Roll 13 Edward I) Harlech was created a borough and the constable of the Castle was appointed *ex officio* mayor of the 'town and liberty'.

Hugh de Longslow was succeeded in the twin offices of Constable and Mayor by John de Benillarde (or Benelared) pursuant to a commission dated 3 October 1285. The new Constable was accompanied by his wife Agnes, and it was she who handed over custody of the virtually completed Castle to the third Constable, James de St George, in July 1290. James de St George, a Savoyard, was the Castle's architect and it remains a monument to his skill and to the ruthlessness of his master, Edward I. The Castle's most distinctive feature is the massive keep-like Gate House on the eastern and most vulnerable side of the structure. There is evidence also that overhangs were created on the castle rock in order to make scaling operations by would-be attackers practically impossible, rather than just extremely difficult. The Castle was designed, of course, first and foremost as a fortress and any internal embellishments were strictly secondary.

The Pipe Roll of 19 Edward I, which covers the period from 30 December 1286 to 27 December 1291, indicates that a total of £8,392 9s 7¾d was spent on construction work at Harlech:

December 1286 to September 1287	£1943	9	6
September 1287 to November 1288	£3436	18	4
November 1288 to December 1289	£914	17	2
December 1289 to December 1290	£1877	1	3¼
December 1290 to December 1291	£220	3	4½

Adding to this the cost of the rock-cut ditch and other preliminary works, the total expenditure on the fortress would have left little change from £10,000, a huge sum at the time. During the most intensive phase of construction, the workforce comprised 227 masons, 115 quarriers, 30 smiths, 22 carpenters and 546 labourers and minor workmen — some 940 men in all. Ships brought limestone from Anglesey and Caernarfon, freestone from Egryn (some seven miles to the south of Harlech) and iron from Chester. A 'Water Gate' was built at the foot of the castle rock.

So, in July 1290, James de St George received the keys of the Castle from Agnes de Benillarde, the widow of his predecessor, John de Benillarde, who had died at Harlech as Constable. No large costs were incurred after 1291. James de St George remained Constable until December 1293, when he was succeeded by Robert de Staundon, on the eve of the new Castle's first military engagement.

The Castle was first tested during the rising of Madog ap Llywelyn, son of Llywelyn ap Maredudd, the last Lord of Ardudwy, in 1294-5, but the fortress withstood his siege. Robert de Staundon had been granted £40 for the custody of the Castle in 1293 but it seems that his brother, Vivian de Staundon, was Constable in 1294-5, and he retained that office in 1303. Another brother, John de Staundon, was a member of the garrison at the time of the rising (as was Thomas de Staundon). Reinforcements were rushed to Harlech at Michaelmas 1294 under Robert de Staundon, and John de Havering brought in seven more men soon afterwards. The reinforced garrison included Hugo Capellanus (chaplain), Matheus portarius (porter), Willelmus pistor (miller), Thomas le Taylour (tailor), Hugo Tinctor (painter) and Ricardus faber (smith). Three of the men brought in by Robert de Staundon at Michaelmas died soon after their arrival at Harlech and one of them appears to have been a Welshman 'David duy' (*du* = black), Black David. One of John de Havering's men was listed, in a contemporary document, as 'Adam de Keyrdif' (Caerdydd or Cardiff, no doubt). The people of Harlech who were recorded in 1294-5 number just 82, and of these 44 were inhabitants of the town: 11 men, 12 women and 21 children. These were the townsmen ('Homines de villa de Hardelach'): Adam Boynard, Madocus crak', Simon le Rede, Ricardus de Oswaldestre (Oswestry), Johannes Sutor, Johannes carbonarius (*alias* John or Ieuan le Colier), Johannes Devenich, Robertus stot, Ricardus bach, Adam 'garcio Johannes le coliere' (John le Colier's boy or son) and Ricardus Boynard. It will be seen that the townsmen included two Welshmen at least — Madocus crak' and Ricardus bach (Little Richard). The women and children were simply numbered, unfortunately. The townspeople certainly had need of their fortress in a hostile Welsh countryside and none more so, perhaps, than the two Welsh interlopers. Soon after this episode Scots captured in battle at Dunbar were imprisoned at Harlech.

Beaumaris castle on Anglesey was built as a direct consequence of Madog's rising and Edward I's ring of fortresses in Gwynedd was thus completed. The alarmed occupiers of Harlech then began to settle in and to exercise their chartered privileges.

The creation of boroughs in Gwynedd was an integral part of Edward I's policy. Some of the new towns were impressively walled, as were Caernarfon and Conwy, but in regard to the lesser towns of Harlech and Criccieth the colonists had to rely upon the castles alone for their protection. Welshmen and Jews were excluded from the enjoyment of burghal privileges and principally from the holding of lands (burgages) within the boroughs. This exclusion policy worked quite effectively at Caernarfon and Conwy, but from a relatively early stage it was not strictly adhered to in the unwalled boroughs of Harlech and Criccieth. In these smaller boroughs the colonisers were themselves colonised, and the more prominent native families, at least, acquired a tincture of Anglo-Norman blood in the process. A number of these families became the leading gentry of the Tudor period. However, the process of assimilation was gradual and was virtually complete by the late 17th century, when the social configuration of Gwynedd was quite well established.

In the late 13th century Harlech could scarcely have been an attractive location for potential colonists, especially since the broad acres of Ireland beckoned. Harlech's charter of 1284 provided a modest patrimony for the Anglo-Norman settlers in the form of lands, certain court perquisites and various economic privileges, but the town's unfavourable location from an economic and commercial point of view concerned the townsmen greatly. As an unwalled town, the borough's territorial extent was never clearly defined. Any boundary stones or other markers have long since disappeared, either physically or from the popular memory, but the borough of Harlech was undoubtedly small and it may not have extended quite literally beyond a stone's throw of the Castle. Older inhabitants still speak of *Penuchardre* or 'Top y dref' (the top of the town) at Penybryn, up what is now called Lion Hill, and they also refer to 'y pentref' (Pentre'r Efail), or the village, which may have been the Welshry, just beyond the borough, in former times. Within the borough, land was held by burgage tenure. By 1312, Harlech contained 29¼ burgages at annual rentals of 12d each which were payable, in equal instalments, at Michaelmas and Easter, to the Royal exchequer at Caernarfon. This alone indicates the smallness of the borough for, in the same year, Caernarfon contained 63 burgages, Conwy 124, Beaumaris 141½, Bala 53 and Criccieth 23⅚. In addition, the burgesses (none of them Welsh at this stage) possessed 123 acres of arable land at 1d per acre. These lands and other privileges (including the income from weekly markets and annual fairs plus court perquisites, all of which involved payments to Caernarfon until 1316) were deemed by the townsmen to be insufficient, so they sought Edward II's bounty and they were not entirely disappointed. On 10 February 1315, the burgesses received a grant of the borough plus the Royal mills and Royal lands in Ardudwy, during the King's pleasure, in return for an annual rental of £19·18s 0½d. However, at the request of the burgesses, on 8 November 1316, Edward II converted the prior grant into one of 'fee-farm' at an annual rental of £22 for ever (Originalia Rolls, 10 Edw II m8). Court perquisites and tolls from annual fairs and weekly markets were merged in this grant of 1316 so that the income from these sources ceased to be a matter of Royal record. In fact, the burgesses paid somewhat over £18 rather than £22 per annum to the exchequer at Caernarfon as a further recognition of their precarious economic position. The grant in fee-farm did not quite conclude the matter. During the next six years a contest was waged between the bailiffs of Harlech, as representatives of the burgesses, and the local ministers of the principality regarding the exact definition of Crown lands in Ardudwy. This contest was won eventually by the bailiffs. The disputed lands included detached arable plots in the 'vills' of Trawsfynydd, Maentwrog, Ffestiniog, Llandecwyn, Llanenddwyn, Llanddwywe and Llanaber plus the uplands of 'Nancoyl' (Nantcol, at the head of Cwm Nantcol at Drws Ardudwy) and a pasture called 'Glasenys' (Lasynys), a rocky island outcrop on the Morfa to the north of the town. Thereafter the burgesses of Harlech added no further lands to their charge save, perhaps, for tracts reclaimed from the Morfa or Harlech Marsh. Many parcels of lands beyond the borough were leased by the bailiffs and burgesses in the reign of Elizabeth I and were later added to the expanding estates of the emergent gentry and were thus lost by the town.

So the 'Harlech Marsh' or 'Great Marsh' (Morfa Harlech), both below and to the north of the Castle formed part of the town's patrimony by the early 14th century, as did the profits of the Royal corn mills in Ardudwy. According to an extent of 1420 (the report of an inquiry into land tenures) there were three Royal mills or 'King's Mills' in the district, to which people of the various parishes were obliged to take their corn to be ground (the duty was called 'suit of mill'): the mill at Harlech served by a mill pond on the northern edge of the castle green (Maesgwyn); the mill at Taltreuddyn near Llanbedr three miles or so to the south of the town; and 'Melin-y-Brenin' (King's Mill) at Dyffryn Ardudwy, the only one of the three to retain its ancient title in modern times. The feudal principle of 'suit of mill' was certainly a fertile source of resentment so far as the Welsh inhabitants of Ardudwy were concerned, since it was a form of monopoly for the benefit of the alien burgesses. In addition, millers were among the most unpopular figures in the Welsh, as in the English countryside during the middle ages, due mainly to their penchant for giving short measure. Illegal hand mills were probably used in the district in an attempt to avoid the official exactions, though discovery meant destruction of the offending hand mill and a heavy fine.

The area of economic and jurisdictional privileges granted in the Charter of 1284 to Harlech, in common with the borough of Criccieth, was deemed to extend from the river Seiont at Caernarfon to the river Dyfi (*ie:* to the southern limit of the county of Merioneth and the traditional boundary between north and south Wales), but there is good reason to believe that, for practical purposes, the burgesses of Harlech were unable to enforce their claims effectively beyond the confines of Ardudwy. This meant that the townsmen asserted a local monopoly over the holding of markets and fairs and claimed certain dues in respect of maritime trade. They also asserted various rights with regard to the holding of courts and the exaction of fines. With reference to maritime trade, it seems that the townsmen claimed a Winchester measure of all grain and salt imported at three landing places in Ardudwy: 'Y Gamlas', on the Dwyryd estuary to the north of the town; 'Traeth Artro' or Mochres (Mochras) near the centre of Ardudwy's coastline; and at Barmouth (Abermaw or Bermo).

Although the Welsh people of Ardudwy retained their tribal lands (the main customary tenures were the *gwely* and the *gafael* as recorded in Extents of 1298 and 1420), their burdens, including taxes and other exactions, increased quite markedly after the conquest. They were, for example, obliged to contribute towards the maintenance of Harlech Castle and the provisioning of its garrison. These and other grievances mounted during the 14th century. In 1332, one Walter de Manny (Mauny) was appointed Constable/Mayor of Harlech for life. He died in 1372 and there is no evidence that he ever set foot in Wales, let alone visited Harlech. This was typical of colonial administration. Many if not most public offices of any consequence in Wales were sinecures, and the duties which attached to them were expected to be performed by deputies. Wales also became a prime source of soldiery, bowmen from south Wales and pikemen from the north, for Edward III's costly wars in France. Pliant Welshmen took full advantage of the situation wherever possible, though they were seldom granted offices of any real importance.

During the 1340s the Black Death or bubonic plague spread into Wales, and several people succumbed at Harlech. They may have been buried near the Castle, as several skeletons, in unmarked graves and without coffins of wood or stone, were uncovered when tan pits were dug there in the early 19th century. This burial ground was associated with an ancient chapel, dedicated to Mary Magdalen, which was used by the burgesses and their families in preferences to the parish church of Llandanwg which lies near the seashore, some two miles to the south of the town. The Constables, or their deputies, had their own small chapel in the Gate House of the Castle, whilst the garrison chapel, for the common soldiery, lay in the Inner Ward of the fortress, within the Castle's northern wall. The Magdalen Chapel probably went out of use in the 16th century, as distinctions between the inhabitants of the town and the people of the district became steadily more social rather than ethnic, but Llandanwg church's location at such a distance from the town continued to discourage regular attendance.

In 1370 an invasion from France commanded by a Welshman, Owain Lawgoch (Red Hand), was anticipated. The garrison at Harlech, like others throughout Wales, was placed on alert but, to the disappointment of many in Wales, no invasion took place. Another Owain was to give expression to the deep and abiding resentments of the Welsh people who had been ground, for so long, between the upper grindstone of alien misrule and exploitation and the nether stone of Welsh quisling opportunism. At Harlech, in the meantime, the burgesses sought to make the most of their patrimony, as did the Welsh inhabitants of Ardudwy on their tribal or family holdings. Retribution drew steadily nearer as a dispute between Owain Glyndŵr and Lord Grey of Ruthin in north-east Wales approached its flash-point.

Owain Glyndŵr raised his standard as Prince of Wales in 1399, and thus declared his opposition to the usurper Henry IV and his son Henry (Shakespeare's Prince Hal), the reputed Prince of Wales as heir to the throne of England, which his father had acquired by murder of Richard II. A Welsh border squabble was soon converted into something akin to a national uprising. Welshmen flocked to join the rising from England (some were students at Oxford and Cambridge) and from the continental mainland. As a sign of the times, the burgesses of Harlech ceased to pay their fee-farm rent from 1399 onwards. Gwynedd rose against its masters of misrule, both alien and native, so the struggle was certainly not devoid of internecine elements. Many old scores were bloodily repaid. Owain is said to have killed his kinsman, Hywel Sele of Nannau near Dolgellau, a quisling, and to have unceremoniously stuffed his corpse into a hollow oak tree (*Ceubren yr Ellyll*).

The Constable of Harlech in 1399 was Richard (Dicon) Mascy, who had been appointed by the putative Prince of Wales in that year (1 Hen IV). Records indicate that the Castle had been kept in reasonably good repair since its completion, and following the rising of Madog ap Llywelyn in 1294-5. Small repairs had been made to the roofs and towers in 1298 and 2,000 shingles had been bought in 1301 for roofing buildings within the fortress. An account of 1319 shows that some of the towers had been provided with new lead roofs, and that the others had been repaired. Two surveys of Royal castles in north Wales, of 1321 and 1343, provide a good deal of information as to maintenance. The latter is the more detailed and this put the cost of repairs at Harlech at £50 6s 0d. It illustrates just how quickly such structures could decay. Repairs to the Great Hall required an outlay of 40s and the chapel (probably the garrison chapel) was then said to be 'weak and ruinous'. The chapel needed 10s in masonry, £3 in woodwork and 40s in lead and other materials. It also gives the original names of some of the towers: the Prison Tower (NE), the 'Gemel' Tower (the Gate House) and the Weathercock Tower (SE). The 'Gemel' Tower needed 46s 8d in masonry, 29s 4d in woodwork and £10 in lead and other materials. The Ystumgwern Hall, also needed some attention. This wooden hall was later burned and only the foundation stones can be seen today. So the Castle was kept in a fair state of readiness to counter any insurrection or possible seaborne invasion. The defences were soon to be tested in the early 15th century.

When the Castle fell to Welsh insurgents in 1404 William Hunte was said to have been Constable, but he seems to have merely led members of the garrison who were anxious to surrender. It is recorded that, in January 1404, William Hunte 'came oute of the Castel for to trete with the Rebell, without any ostage [hostage] laede in for hym. And the same tyme Robin of Holond [commander of the insurgents], and other with hym, the which toke Jankyn Euor, laede honde [hand] upon the said William & lad hym awae, & too zemen [the men] with him; one Jak Mercer, & that othir Harry Baker . . . what they did with hem I connot sae at this tyme'. Yet surrender of the Castle was delayed by the continued defiance of Vivian ('Fivean') Collier, a leading townsman and descendant of the first John or Ieuan le Col(1)ier, and a certain 'Sir Lewes' (Lewis). When Hunte was captured, the garrison consisted of just five Englishmen and fifteen Welshmen, though earlier it had comprised the Constable (or his deputy), ten men-at-arms and thirty archers. Owain Glyndŵr negotiated the surrender in person and the stubborn remnant were, it seems, allowed to go unpunished. With the fall of the Castle, Harlech became Owain Glyndŵr's headquarters or capital, and remained so for some four years. A parliament is said to have been convened in this period at Tŷ Mawr in Harlech, a large house which survived until the late 19th century (by then in a ruinous condition). The ruin was then replaced by two houses, one of which retained the old name 'Tŷ Mawr' (Big House) and the other named, appropriately enough, 'Glyndŵr'. Envoys from France also came to Harlech so that, for a few years, the small town was at the very centre of independent Welsh affairs. Here, for example, Owain was able to give thought to his plan for the creation of universities in north and south Wales.

On the other hand, the Welsh insurgents burned no less than 46 houses, and household goods and other effects to the value of 500 marks were said to have been carried off or destroyed. The true extent of the damage may have been exaggerated, since the details were recorded in subsequent claims (possibly deliberately inflated) for compensation, but the Welsh had no reason to let the haughty burgesses of Harlech off lightly. John or Ieuan Col(l)ier, head of the leading burghal family, was relieved of 165 head of cattle, 40 horses, 100 sheep and 100 goats, together with goods to the value of £50. His brother Vivian lost 40 cattle, while five other burgesses, all bearing English surnames, were deprived, or so it was said, of 150 beasts. This tells us something about the town's economy, *ie:* the burgesses, like the Welsh of Ardudwy, were mainly pastoralists.

Robin Holland of Eglwys Fach, who led the attack, may have left his memorial here in the name 'Muriau Hol(l)and' (Holland's Walls), a name which still denoted a central portion of the town in the mid-19th century. The Marcher lord, Edmund Mortimer, Owain Glyndŵr's son-in-law, died at Harlech (he is commemorated in the Castle's 'Mortimer Tower') and Owain's wife, daughter and four grandchildren were captured when the Castle was taken for Henry IV by the Talbot brothers in 1408-9 with a force of 1,000 men. Owain Glyndŵr escaped to wage a brilliant but ultimately futile guerilla campaign and died, it is believed, in 1415. His son, Maredudd ab Owain, also avoided capture, and continued his defiance in Merioneth between 1410 and 1421.

Harlech Castle was surrendered to the Talbots in 1408-9. Two incidents during the siege deserve a brief recital. On 23 January 1415, two petitions were heard by Henry V in Council. One was a claim by Gerard Sprong for payment in respect of the metal used in the manufacture of a brass cannon, called the 'Kinges Doughtir' (King's Daughter), which had burst at the siege of Harlech. Sprong also sought compensation for a cannon, called the 'Messager' (Messenger), weighing 4,480 lbs, which had burst at the siege of Aberystwyth. The answer was that 'The King grants all as be requests', since English monarchs acknowledged no contractual obligations for services rendered, though subjects could petition for compensation as a matter of grace and favour. The other petition related to the capture of a vessel, by the Welsh, at or near Harlech, during the siege of the Castle in 1408-9. John Horne, a citizen and fishmonger of London, claimed that his vessel, laden with provisions, was arrested for the service (*ie:* commandeered) by Lords Talbot and Furnival and their soldiers engaged in the siege. Gilbert Talbot certified that the siege would have failed in the absence of supplies (which suggests that other vessels completed their missions). The report continued:

'. . . when he [Horne] arrived there, and had partly unladen the provisions, and received payment for them, the "Welsh Rebels" came upon him and seized the money which he had received and the remainder of the provisions in the said vessel and moreover, burnt the ship, took him prisoner and fixed his ransom at twenty marks; which provisions, money, ship and ransom was of the value of upwards of 100 marks.'

Henry V also granted this petition.

The rising of Owain Glyndŵr and the code of repressive laws enacted by the English Parliament in response to it meant that Harlech remained a garrison town for some time to come. Any easing of the relationship between the townsmen and the people of Ardudwy was probably reversed, as both sides licked their wounds and contemplated each other with mutual suspicion if not outright hostility. An Extent of survey of land tenures in Ardudwy and other districts of 1420 was a response to Owain Glyndŵr's evident desire and purpose to destroy all records of subjection to alien rule. In Ardudwy, traditional Welsh tenures, based upon partible inheritance, still predominated, and the Norman principle of primogeniture (the legal presumption in favour of the eldest son with regard to the descent of landed property) had made little if any headway in this Welsh fastness. There were two main forms of traditional tenure: the *gafael* (as in the Kentish custom of 'gavelkind') and the *gwely*. One *gafael* recorded in 1420 deserves notice since it was named after a woman — *Gafael Gwenllian Dew* (Fat Gwenllian's Gafael), situated at Dyffryn Ardudwy. The native gentry were to change all this as they began to claw their way to power and preferment during the next two centuries or so, for the Norman principle suited their designs.

Owain Glyndŵr's son Maredudd and his confederates surrendered in south Merioneth in 1421 and were pardoned for their past 'transgressions', but for the Welsh people generally, Royal exactions and other features of misrule were thoroughly restored. In 1446 the annual fee-farm rent was again paid by the townsmen of Harlech to the exchequer at Caernarfon after a lapse of some 47 years. This, coupled with Royal compliance, suggests the virtual devastation of the town and its fragile economy then. Subject to a few possible exceptions, the 46 houses which were said to have been burned by the Welsh insurgents were never rebuilt, though some may have been rendered fit for human habitation according to the rude standards of the time. The Castle at Criccieth was so much damaged by the Welsh that no attempt was ever made to restore it. At Harlech, the expropriators had been themselves expropriated, but the sight of such cannons as the 'Kinges Doughtir' must have helped to restore their dented confidence, even as they and superior ordnance threatened the castles with redundancy.

There is a tradition that Queen Margaret of Anjou, consort of the imprisoned and pathetic Henry VI, came into Wales with her son Prince Edward, after the battle of Towton, and that she came to Harlech where she appointed Dafydd ab Ieuan ab Einion Constable of the Castle in her own name and those of her husband and son. Be this as it may, Dafydd was the first Welsh Constable of Harlech and the garrison at the time, in 1461, was composed largely of his kinsmen, who were members of emergent gentry families of the district. They were named in the following petition of the 'Tenants and Commons of North Wales' addressed to the first Parliament of the Yorkist Edward IV in 1461:

'Where many and divers of them have been daily taken prisoners and put to fine and ransom as it were in land or war; and many and divers of them daily robbed and spoiled of their goods and cattle contrary to the law by David ap Ieuan ap Eynon, Griffith Vaughan ap Griffith ap Eynon, Jenkyn ap Iorwerth ap Eynon, Thomas ap Ieuan ap Eynon, Griffith ap Ieuan ap

Eynon, John ap Ieuan ap Eynon, John Hanmer, Morys ap David ap Griffith, David ap Ieuan ap Owen, David ap Eynon ap Ieuan, Grommys ap Ieuan ap Eynon ap Ieuan, Grommys ap Howel ap Morgan, Edward ap Morgan, John Tother, clerk, Griffith ap Ieuan ap Iorwerth, and Rheinallt ap Griffith ap Bleddyn, and Morys Robert . . .'

This then was a proud company of Welshmen asserting themselves in their own land, albeit under Lancastrian warrant and probably to their own material advantage, and one which, despite the plethora of names, comprised just 17 'well born' men. The petitioners went on to complain:

'. . . and over more the said David ap Eynon calleth himself by the name of Constable of Harlech, and that he kepeth it to the use and behove of him that he calleth his sovereign lord King Henry VI, saying as well by his mouth as by his writing that the said castle was committed to him by his sovereign lord aforesaid and by his sovereign lady Queen Margaret and his right and gracious lord Prince Edward, and sworn to keep it to their use and will not deliver it to no other saving to such as one of them shall assign, notwithstanding the King's commandment is the contrary. And daily the said David and all the aforesaid misdoers take and repute in all their demeanour the said late king for their sovereign lord and not the king our sovereign lord that now is as their duty is. And moreover all the said misdoers taketh oxen, sheep, wheat, and victuals of the said poor tenants for stuff of the said castle with strong hand and will not deliver it to no person as the late King hath deputed to be his constable there.'

Most of Merioneth's leading Welsh families appear to have supported the Lancastrian cause several years before Henry Tudor became the faction's claimant to the English throne. For example, my kinsman Dafydd Llwyd of Cwm Bychan, a harpist and soldier, was an early adherent. He is believed to have been executed, with Owen Tudor, after the battle of Mortimer's Cross in 1461. His main memorial is the melody or air (*alaw*) 'Ffarwel Dai Llwyd'. His death was probably avenged by kinsmen at Bosworth in 1485. What was generally in England a squalid and murderous dynastic struggle became, in many parts of Wales, a truly patriotic conflict wreathed in the romance of a second King Arthur. Henry Tudor and his advisers derived considerable advantage from this theme. However, due to the pernicious influence of the warring factions in Wales, where Yorkists dominated in the south and Lancastrians in the north (with additional complications in the Marches of Wales), Welshmen fought on both sides at least until the struggle reached its momentous climax in 1485.

So Dafydd ab Ieuan ab Einion was Queen Margaret of Anjou's champion at Harlech in 1461 (she soon went to Lorraine, however), though his tenure of the office of Constable of the Castle is open to some doubt. In 1464, William, Lord Herbert, a Cambro-Norman of south Wales, was appointed Constable of Harlech for life by a peevish Edward IV, and this Yorkist monarch instructed him to lay waste extensive tracts of Gwynedd and to assert his commission at Harlech. Lord Herbert's march through Gwynedd was one of the most savage episodes of the bitter and protracted conflict. A contemporary chronicler penned this brief account in 'Y Llyfr Gwyn' (The White Book):

'A° 1468 y daeth arglwydd Herbert i Wynedd dan ladd a llosgi a chodi dyfawr dreth ar bob Cwmwd y Gwynedd ar Gwmwd y Penllyn [In the year 1468 Lord Herbert came to Gwynedd and subjected it to killing and burning and the exaction of great fines throughout every district of Gwynedd and the district of Penllyn].'

This fine example of late mediaeval chivalry made war on old men, women and children with nothing short of Cromwellian ferocity.

After a spirited defence, Harlech Castle was surrendered in 1468 to Sir Richard Herbert of Coalbrookdale, Lord Herbert's younger brother. It was the last castle surrendered to the Yorkists (on 14 August 1468). Legend has it that Edward IV insisted upon Dafydd ab Ieuan ab Einion's execution and that Sir Richard refused and threatened to hand back the Castle to its gallant defender. Another story relates to a boast, allegedly made, at some point by Dafydd, that he had kept a castle in France so long that the old women of Wales came to hear of it, and that he would keep this castle in Wales until the old women of France knew of it. There is no direct evidence that Dafydd remained at Harlech in 1468, *ie* some seven years after his initial commission, but the defence of the Castle continues to be ascribed to Dafydd ab Ieuan ab Einion.

Yet another story of that time is that Henry Tudor himself was captured at Harlech, and that William Herbert attempted to marry him to his daughter Maud to further his own dynastic ambitions. Harlech was considered to be the headquarters of Jasper Tudor, a half-brother of Henry VI and uncle of young Henry Tudor. What is certain is that, on 8 September 1468, Lord Herbert, the high-born butcher of Gwynedd's people, was created Earl of Pembroke following the attainer of Jasper Tudor. However, he did not live long to enjoy his new title and its perquisites, since he was killed at the battle of Banbury in 1469.

For the people of Harlech and Ardudwy the Castle had again attracted conflict and devastation, and in 1468 peace and stability still seemed a long way off. Edward I's legacy was a distinctly bitter one. Yet, centuries later, the defence of the Castle in 1468 was to be immortalised in what was to become the world famous 'March of the Men of Harlech' (*Rhyfelgyrch Gwŷr Harlech*). This was first published by Edward Jones (*Bardd y Brenin*) in 1784 in his *Musical and Poetical Relicks of the Welsh Bards*. The most memorable Welsh words of this 'war song' were composed by John Ceiriog Hughes (*Ceiriog*) in about 1860: 'Wele goelcerth wen yn fflamio, a thafodau tân yn bloeddio . . .' Their lyricism would be lost in translation.

Between 1468 and 1485 the Lancastrian interest was advanced clandestinely throughout Wales, as that interest was welded to the ambitions of the House of Tudor. Gruffydd Fychan (Vaughan) of Corsygedol in Ardudwy built a tower house at Abermaw (Barmouth), Tŷ Gwyn (White House), which served, it seems, to maintain communications between north and south Wales at that sequestered spot on behalf of the Tudors. When Henry Tudor landed at Dale in Pembrokeshire and marched through Wales *en route* to Bosworth Field, one of the contingents which joined his growing army came from Corsygedol. Gruffydd Fychan was rewarded for his service with the governorship of Cilgerran Castle, an office which passed to his son, William Vaughan. The influence of this family in Ardudwy and in Merioneth increased steadily in the Tudor period.

The battle of Bosworth and the death of Richard III placed Henry Tudor on the English throne and, in Wales, actively promoted prophecies of the coming of a second Arthur appeared to have been realised (Henry VII named his eldest son Arthur). The penal laws of the Glyndŵr period were repealed. Welshmen flocked to London like starlings, where several rose high in the service of the new dynasty. Henry VII was certainly not unmindful of his partly Welsh descent and of the vital support given to his cause in Wales. The emergent gentry of Wales set about consolidating and extending their estates as Henry VII was doing much the same for his Kingdom. The gentry of Wales also began quite steadily to adopt English speech and manners, though the pace varied from district to district, and nowhere was it more gradual than in Ardudwy. Mansions were built or rebuilt and enlarged (especially during the reign of Elizabeth I) and several churches in Ardudwy, as elsewhere, were rebuilt and embellished (local examples include the churches at Llanfair and Llanddwywe or Talybont). Harlech's parish church remained the church at Llandanwg, situated some two miles from the town, whereas the chapel dedicated to Mary Magdalen at Harlech probably fell into disuse either before or immediately after the Reformation under Henry VIII. The 'Tudor Peace' was a time of rebuilding, discernible economic advance and of growing confidence after the ravages of the 15th century. It was also a period of increasing social stratification and of the ruthless exploitation of the weak by the strong. Attempts were made, particularly under the direction of Rowland Lee, to curb the worst excesses of the gentry in Wales but, all the while, the fortunes of several families were advanced by a more or less deft mixture of suitable marriages, corruption, legal chicanery and outright violence. Respectability descended upon them in the course of the 17th century (they also became much less inbred) but the nefarious activities of the gentry in Ardudwy as elsewhere are reflected in the records of the Court of Star Chamber and the Council of Wales and the Marches. They were the new masters and they missed few opportunities to press this point home upon their hapless countrymen, and their ascendancy continued until at least the mid-19th century. The gentry were the chosen instruments of the 'New Monarchy' and most Tudor policies ministered to their rampant ambitions and not least the Reformation settlement. The advance of the gentry in Ardudwy forms a backdrop to the history of Harlech between 1500 and 1800.

Henry Tudor's victory at Bosworth in 1485, coupled with advancing techniques of warfare, meant that the castles of Wales appeared increasingly irrelevant and needlessly costly. For its part, Harlech Castle began to take on the appearance of a stately ruin. The animosities of former times waned and Harlech ceased to be a garrison town in a hostile Welsh environment. The town was also exposed to much more open economic competition and thereby to the threat of virtual extinction. Merioneth remained a poor county, but Harlech's commercial decline was very much related to the advance of the borough of Bala and the unincorporated town of Dolgellau. Harlech's status as a borough and as the county town of Merioneth became increasingly illusory as mediaeval protectionism was withdrawn. In other words, Harlech had been well chosen as the site for a castle but as an administrative and commercial centre the town could not compete effectively with its main rivals.

OPPOSITE: Tŷ'r Eiddew (Ivy Cottage) which occupies the site of the former burgesses's chapel dedicated to Mary Magdalen. ABOVE: Llandanwg church with its bell. The east window must once have been quite fine. (GAS) BELOW: The ruins of old Tŷ Mawr, Harlech, where Glyndŵr is said to have held a parliament in the early 15th century. (JH/GAS)

Harlech as recorded in the Tithe Map of Llandanwg parish, 1840. Some of the small enclosures may have been remnants of ancient burgages. (NLW)

Key: 594 Penybryn; 687 Muriau Holland (Holland's Walls); 701 Tan-y-Castell (part of the Blue Lion farm); 705/715 Gerddi Twtil (Toothill Gardens); 711 Clogwyn-y-Capel; 716 Gardd-y-Castell (the Castle Garden); 717 Maesgwyn or the Castle Green; 718 Shire/Town Hall; 719 White Horse; 720 Maesgwyn houses; 725 Blue Lion Inn; 726 St Tanwg's Church; 730 Gardd-yr Efail (the Smithy garden); 768/769 Cae Besi. Harlech's principal landowners in 1840 were Sir R. W. Vaughan of Nannau, William Ormsby Gore, Esq., of Glyn Cywarch and the Hon. E. M. Ll. Mostyn of Corsygedol. Note the large Morfa Allotments below the town under the Enclosure Act of 1806.

LEFT: A gilt bronze boss from the martingale of a set of horse harness bearing the arms of Owain Glyndŵr as prince of Wales, discovered in the Castle in 1923. RIGHT: The main entrance to Tŷ Mawr, Harlech, c1890. (JH/GAS) BELOW: Tŷ Gwyn, Barmouth (left corner) in the early 20th century. Originally a 'tower house', it served as a centre of Lancastrian intrigue between 1468 and 1485.

ABOVE: Part of a lease of town lands in the 16th century by the bailiffs and burgesses of Harlech with the Common Seal affixed. (GAS) BELOW: A section of the Speede map of Merioneth, 1610, indicating the three inlets over which Harlech claimed some jurisdiction in 1650 pursuant to the charter. (CH)

In Decline

By 1500 Harlech was a town by Royal charter, its location determined by military considerations. The site had little to commend it in most other respects, particularly since communications within the corrugated county of Merioneth were notoriously bad, and remained so until at least the 19th century. The relative stability which developed under the early Tudors steadily eroded Harlech's military significance. Relations between the townspeople and the district's Welsh inhabitants gradually mellowed as the former were assimilated by the latter. The town, particularly due to its smallness and the absence of town walls, was cambricised or cymricised and the 'union' of England and Wales effected under Henry VIII by Acts of 1536 and 1543 emphasised the virtual redundancy of the castles of Edward I. This is not to ignore the tensions produced by the Henrican Reformation, which meant that Harlech and other castles in Gwynedd, as elsewhere, were maintained in some state of readiness in case of possible invasion by the Catholic powers of Europe, but the Castle's original *raison d'être* became scarcely more than a vague memory and Harlech's weak economic position was exposed increasingly during the 16th and 17th centuries.

Since the castles of Gwynedd no longer served to impress a colonial regime upon a subject people, they were allowed to decay. The Henrican Reformation placed no significant strain on Welsh loyalty to the Tudors, and the Acts of Union of 1536 and 1543 were welcomed by the gentry and accepted by the Welsh people at large. A newly defined Wales was effectively annexed to England though special courts, the Courts of Great Sessions, were established for Wales (exclusive of Monmouthshire) and the Council of Wales and the Marches, with headquarters at Ludlow, exercised general administrative control. On the other hand, the Welsh language was denied public status and was to be 'extirped' by legislative decree. In general, English institutions were extended to Wales. Harlech Castle remained an impressive structure, but a survey, dated 23 September 1564, indicates the steady onset of decay. Reference was made to the castle green (Maesgwyn), which had allowed a clear field of fire for the defenders and no cover in the way of buildings for attackers, which was said to extend from Ffynnon Fair (Mary's Well) to 'toothill' (*Twtil*). This green was some 30 roods long and four roods wide. Access to the Castle was by way of a bridge which spanned the ditch (it was never a moat): 'The Bridge, Consisteth of an Arch of Stone, rising from the bottom of the diche, battlemented on both sides, in the midds between the Grene and the Castle, ye distaunce now fulfilled with tymber and plank, in great Decaye, where have bene two Drawen Bridges — in length xxx yerdes bredth iiij yerdes'. The Gate House alone was in reasonably good repair, since this was used to accommodate the justices of the Great Sessions when they came to this county town: 'The Gate House, Consisting of twoo greate towres towards the bridge, two turretts towards the inner Courte [the Inner Ward], being vices [winding staircases] onlie, and other buildings, as followeth: with also ii great gates, get in good

Reparacion, with a port cullys'. Within the castle was 'a stately stayre' [stair] leading from the inner courts in the Gate House of 30 'grises' or steps. The lead on all the towers was 'greatlie decayed' though the ramparts were described as being 'stronglie walled, & battlemented, founded vppon the rocke environing the Castle'. Reference was also made to the Debtors' Tower, which was probably still in use as a debtors' prison. These civil or civilian uses of the Castle — as a lodging for judges and a prison for debtors — required some maintenance. In fact, the Castle was to be the townsmen's one true bargaining point in their attempts to retain the Great Sessions and the county Quarter Sessions in the face of increasing competition from Dolgellau and Bala in the early 17th century. The survey of 1564 suggests that the Castle could still have been defended in spite of general decay, but further military use was not seriously contemplated.

The linked offices of Constable of the Castle and Mayor remained sinecures throughout the Tudor period and these principal offices were invariably granted to outsiders. On 1 November 1485, the offices of Constable and Mayor were confirmed, by Act of Parliament, to Piers Stanley and to Richard Pole, a 'Squire of the King's Body'. They were either appointed jointly or in succession. Richard Pole remained Constable and Mayor on 29 December 1500, by which time he had been knighted. In fact, the grant of 1485 appears to have been cancelled in 1495 and replaced by a re-grant to Richard Pole in that year. In a deed of 1529 (21 Henry VIII), Edward Stanley was represented as Mayor and Deputy-Constable of Harlech, but it seems that he was deputy in both offices to Sir Francis Bryan, who was Constable from 1521. Yet Edward Stanley became MP for Merioneth and he was later appointed Constable of Harlech in 1551 (26 March, 5 Edward VI). Sir Anthony Strelley, of the county of Nottingham, was Constable between 1558 and 1576. On 5 February 1589 (31 Elizabeth I), Sir Henry Lee and Owen Cooke, Gent, were granted the twin offices to hold 'successive' during their lives and the life of the survivor. Lee held both offices until he died in 1611, by which time he was a Knight of the Garter. There is no reason to believe that Sir Henry Lee spent much time at Harlech since his home was in Kent. While he was Constable and Mayor he sought to gain as much land as he possibly could in the neighbourhood. This letter, written by Lee from his home in Ditchley, Kent, in 1609, to Sir William Maurice of Clenennau, who had been elected a bailiff of Harlech, provides some idea of his care and concern for Harlech and of the nature of the man:

'Sr William Morris, I receved a letter from you, I vnderstand thereby that you are chosen one of the Baliffes of Harloughe, wherein I thinke you may stand your good neighbours in some steede [stead]. The repayre of the Kinges Castles are not in my handes. It may be some thinkes, It is a place may be spared, And so to save charges. The last repayre I procured, the allowance was bestowed vpon it. The towne may be less poore, If you have procured them touchinge the land I have in the marshe, you mought have had as much as you now desieyre [desire]. And I do commit you to God.

ffrom ditchley this viijth of ffebruary 1609

Your loveing ffrend

Henry Lee.'

So Lee was not disposed to lift a finger to assist Maurice and his associates at Harlech to secure the repair of the Gate House for the accommodation of the judges, because they had failed to advance his material interests.

The burgesses and their representatives, the bailiffs, who were then members of the local gentry, were concerned about the town's economic decline, but their concern was not public-spirited but simply self-seeking. During the 16th century (certainly between the 1530s and the 1590s) borough lands were leased to various individuals, including members of the principal local gentry families of Corsygedol, Glyn Cywarch, Maesyneuadd and Tanybwlch, by the deputy-mayors, aldermen, bailiffs and burgesses. The lands so leased never reverted to the town but were later incorporated into the gentry estates. These leases, together with the land-grabbing propensities of absentee officials like Sir Henry Lee, resulted in the reduction of the town's patrimony. The decline was thus closely associated with the rise of the gentry. When doubts arose as to the legality of the 16th century leases in the early 17th century, the burgesses sought the opinion of legal counsel in 1611. The original paper was kept at Brogyntyn (Porkington in Shropshire) and was endorsed, probably in the hand of the ubiquitous Sir William Maurice of Clenennau, 'Mr. Noye and Mr. Walter's oppinions touching the chartr of harlech'. By rather different routes the two lawyers reached the same conclusion: that the dealings in borough lands were valid despite the fact that the lessors were not named consistently. Walter deemed that Harlech was a corporation by prescription rather than by grant.

A letter, dated 29 June 1612, written by Griffith Vaughan of Corsygedol Esq, to Sir William Maurice of Clenennau Knt, provides some telling insights into the activities and attitudes of the gentry then. The writer referred to 'those falsh boores of harleghe' by which he meant 'the foure that are oure capitall aduersaries'. It seems that Robert Wynne had taken Harlech's common chest 'with all the charters and writtinges belonging vnto the corporation, from the usuall place where it was kepte before, without ye privitie or assent of any of ye Burgesses' and that he did this with the connivance of his three 'adherents & consortes'. Vaughan had obtained a special warrant, addressed to Robert Lloyd of Rhiwgoch as deputy-mayor of Harlech, to 'breake the lockes, vpon refusall of ye Bailiffes to make serch for certen writtinges supposed to be in ye same chest, touching certen medowes & landes, belonging vnto the constable of ye Castell'. The Constable and Mayor of Harlech then was none other than Sir William Maurice. The gentry's greed for land knew no bounds, and it is not surprising that Harlech suffered. No wonder the original town charter and other paraphernalia were forever lost. And this was by no means all. The early 17th century was remarkable in Merioneth, as elsewhere in Wales, for the lawlessness of the gentry as they contended among themselves for local supremacy. They fought over land, public offices and just about anything which they felt could be turned to personal or family advantage. Star Chamber records are a veritable Burke's *Landed Gentry* of high-born criminality. While the following examples were allegations and not proven offences, they do provide a rancid flavour of the period. Richard Corbett of Llanfor complained that John Vaughan of Glanllyn Tegid (Bala) JP, had denied equal justice to rich and poor; refused justice against his servants; terrorised the Great Inquest (Grand Jury) at the Sessions at Harlech with 500 men upon a bill being preferred against him so that he was acquitted; and Vaughan was further charged with self aggrandisement on pretence of musters. John Wyn ap Griffith complained that Ellis Brynkir had assaulted him at the Sessions of Harlech and at Penmorfa. William Maurice ab Ellis, Sheriff, Rowland ab Ellis, mayor of Bala, and Richard Meyrick, deputy sheriff, were charged, with others, with bribery and corruption at the Great Sessions of Harlech and of a false verdict by David ap Lewis. Pierce Lloyd of Dolau JP, charged Cadwalader Price of Rhiwlas and John Lewis Owen of Llwyn, Dolgellau (a member of a notoriously troublesome family), both of whom were JPs and deputy lieutenants of Merioneth, with several misdemeanours in office: embezzling £1,000 worth of armour at Harlech Castle (probably a grossly inflated estimate of value); illegally taxing the people to make up for the consequent loss; illegally imprisoning those who refused to pay the illegal tax, to the number of 300; mustering for their own enrichment; forcing the election of John Vaughan of Caergai, their kinsman, as MP for Merioneth; and with bribery and corruption as magistrates. When due allowance is made for the florid legal language of these charges, the situation in Merioneth in late Elizabethan and early Jacobean times was certainly unedifying. By the 18th century, however, a veil had been drawn over these intrigues and the grand and lesser gentry became respectable and even responsible leaders of Merioneth society, but by then Harlech was of no real interest to them, since what little remained of corporate or borough status concerned only the humble townsmen, *ie:* the shopkeepers, tradesmen and suchlike. This was because Harlech lost the Great Sessions and Quarter Sessions and thereby the main elements of its county status.

Harlech's decline in the 16th and 17th centuries was not simply a matter of leases of borough lands and various gentry intrigues concerning borough records. Decline was partly due to the town's poor location as a commercial centre. An inquisition into yearly fairs of 1606 indicated the growing commercial importance of Dolgellau, an unincorporated town, and the corresponding eclipse of Harlech. The town's mediaeval economic privileges were no longer effective as a counter to adverse geographic location. By 1606, Harlech had three annual fairs whereas formerly, from 1335, it had had four. Dolgellau had three annual fairs each of which was of greater value than Harlech's or those of Bala. The number of fairs at Harlech was later increased to eight (by the 19th century) but the income remained quite modest. Harlech's location also told against the town with reference to its 'county town' status. Here the general effects of the Acts of Union of 1536 and 1543 must be noticed. The English Common Law (and Equity) was extended to Wales though special circuit courts were created: the Courts of Great Sessions as distinct from the English Assizes. The office of Justice of the Peace was extended to Wales along with various other English offices and institutions, and the magistrates in Quarter Sessions became the administrative agencies of the counties, as in England. Parliamentary representation was accorded to the Welsh counties and to certain boroughs, but the Merioneth boroughs (Harlech, Bala and Bere) were deemed too small and poor to justify either individual or collective representation (as in Caernarfonshire — Caernarfon Boroughs), so Merioneth was granted just a shire MP. This was quite reasonable in the circumstances since the county could not have afforded ampler representation. It did mean, however, that Harlech had no special or regular spokesman in Parliament to protect or promote the town's interests. Furthermore, the administration of Wales from Tudor times until 1689 (save for the period from 1640 to 1660) was supervised by the Council of Wales and the Marches at Ludlow. While this Council has been seen by some historians as a form of devolved government it was really part of a centralising process, since the governance of Gwynedd, for example, had been formerly based on Caernarfon. The justices of Great Sessions operated from Ludlow and those assigned to Merioneth clearly favoured Dolgellau and Bala rather than Harlech.

As the county town of Merioneth, Harlech stood to benefit economically from the holding of the Quarter Sessions, and especially of the Great Sessions in the town, because the Sessions brought large numbers of people, hungry and thirsty for the most part, and thus trade. The local gentry also derived economic benefits, but the holding of the Sessions at Harlech ministered, in addition, to their self-esteem. Competition from Dolgellau and Bala gave rise to mounting concern among the gentry-burgesses and this concern peaked in the early years of the 17th century. What may be called the battle for the Sessions at Harlech ensued.

The effort to retain the Sessions was stepped up in 1604 when the burgesses and their representatives, the bailiffs, all of whom were members of the gentry, sought to enlist the services of Sir William Maurice of Clenennau by means of a bribe of £100 offered to Sir William in this letter, dated 6 June 1604:

'Right worshipfull, our hartie comendations remembered, &c., we are beholdynge to your worship for your paynes and good will towards the poor towne of Hardlech, desiringe you styll contynewe your suit for vs, to use meanes to obtayne the both Sessions, and fower [four] quarter Sessions, to be yeerely kept at Hardlech, by acte of parliment; which if you can

obtaine, and bringe to passe, we the burgises subscribed, are contented & willinge to geve you the some [sum] of money apperinge apon our Severall names, vnder written . . .)'
They signed themselves 'Your assured loving ffrends & kinsmen' and added: 'delieuer this with speed'. The £100 was to include Sir William's expenses 'your paynes & travell'). The burgesses included Griffith Vaughan of Corsygedol, Morris Wynn of Glyn Cywarch, Robert ab Ieuan ap Morgan of Taltreuddyn and Robert Lloyd of Rhiwgoch (Trawsfynydd), all of whom promised to pay Sir William £10 each towards the sum of £100. They also offered a bribe of £50 to Ralph, Lord Eure, Lord President of the Council of Wales and the Marches, at Ludlow. Eure accepted this bribe and seems to have made some attempt to secure the Great and Quarter Sessions for Harlech. Sir William also played his well-paid part. A Bill was prepared and a copy, with Sir William's annotations, survives amongst the Brogyntyn (Porkington) Papers. It is headed: 'Considerations for the kepinge of the sessions, &c., at Harlech'. Sir William noted:

'Imprimis, the said Towne of Harleghe is an Ancient Boroughe, beinge a very poore towne, & no through [thorough] faire place, having no trade, or traphicke nor other means to live, but onlye relieved by havinge hearetofore the Assises and quarter sessiones most comonlye kept there.)

The Castle (and its Gate House) was seen as Harlech's trump card:

'Item, the said Castle beinge, as yet, kepte in somme better reparcion than any of his majesty's castle in Northwalles, by reason that the Justices of ye Assises, Sheriffe, & prenotarye, with their trayne do vse when the assises are kepte in that Towne, to lie and keepe ther diet within the said Castle. At which tyme, the said Castle is aired, scowred, cleansed & some charges bestowed by euery Sheriffe, towards the reparacion thereof, at euery time that they doe vse to resorte thither to keepe the Sessions.'

He also noted that the common gaol of Merioneth was 'vsuallie kepte in the said Towne, and the poor prisoners therein, relieved by the inhabitants thereof'. But what of the opposition? Bala was said to be 'a very fylthie dyrtie Towne, without any lodgings fitt for gentlemen', whilst Dolgellau was not even mentioned. In conclusion, Sir William Maurice observed:

'Item, the said Castle is a faire house, & standeth verye pleasante for all kind of exercise & sports, & may be kept in reparacion by havinge the Sessions and quarter sessions as aforesaid, with very little charge or none vnto the kinge; for the Towne & countrey will helpe to repaire it and ther for it is great pittie to suffer it to decaye, seinge it may so easelie be kept & maintained.'

So ended an intriguing example of 17th century sales promotion! Perhaps Sir William did have a soft spot for Harlech but, in spite of his well-paid efforts, the burgesses lost. The last Quarter Sessions were held at Harlech in about 1669 (the surviving Rolls date from the 18th century) and the last Great Sessions in 1674. Dolgellau secured the Quarter Sessions and shared the Great Sessions (and the Assizes following the abolition of the Welsh Courts of Great Sessions in 1830) with Sir William's 'very fylthie dyrtie Towne' of Bala. Harlech's county status had all but disappeared by the 18th century save for the nomination of candidates and the proclamation of MPs for Merioneth, which continued there until 1874. Harlech's income was considerably reduced along with its status and the local gentry tended to lose interest in the town thereafter until the 19th century. The ancient Shire Hall, which doubled as the Town Hall, situated on the town side of the castle green (Maesgwyn), mouldered, though it continued to be used for county elections, even after it became roofless.

The 'English Civil War' began in 1642. Scotland, Wales and Ireland were much involved in this bitter conflict. Wales was largely Royalist in sympathy under gentry control and provided Royalist infantry to be slaughtered on English battle fields by superior Parliamentary forces, composed of men who possessed some notion, it seems, of what they were fighting for (or against). The Merioneth gentry were staunchly Royalist in sentiment and a number actually fought in the war. Yet the county also possessed at least three notable Parliamentary supporters in Morgan Llwyd (1619-1659) of Cynfal, Maentwrog, Colonel John Jones (1597?-1660) of Maesygarnedd in Cwm Nantcol and Rev John Ellis (?-1665) of Llandecwyn, rector of Dolgellau from 1646 and 1665. All three had been subject to influences outside the conservative county of their birth and early nurture: Morgan Llwyd at Wrexham, John Jones in the sevice, as a kinsman, of the Myddleton family of Chirk and John Ellis at the universities of Cambridge and St Andrew's. Two other prominent persons should be mentioned: Rev John Owen, a descendant of the Owen family of Llwyn near Dolgellau, who was Oliver Cromwell's chaplain; and William Lewis (1592-1667) DD, of Egryn, Llanaber, who was provost of Oriel College, Oxford, and chaplain to the Duke of Buckingham, Lord Chancellor Bacon and Charles I. William Lewis, my kinsman, went into exile following the defeat of Charles I and embraced Catholicism. Even Oliver Cromwell, alias Oliver Williams, had a distant family connection with Merioneth, as a descendant of the Nannau family, the armorial crest of which was the Blue Lion of Cadwgan ap Bleddyn (d1111).

Merioneth possessed no real significance for either side in the Civil War. Despite occasional skirmishes (including an assault on Barmouth from the sea by Cardiganshire Parliamentarians) and troop movements, the Royalist defence and the Parliamentary capture of Harlech Castle proved to be by far the most dramatic local incidents of the war. It was surprising that the Castle was garrisoned at all, since it had neither strategic nor tactical significance. Once garrisoned, however, the Castle became a low priority objective for the Parliamentarians.

In 1644, Colonel William Owen (1607-1670) of Brogyntyn (Porkington) in Shropshire, a relative of Sir William Maurice of Clenennau and brother of Sir John Owen (1600-1660), a Major-General in the Royalist army, wrote to Prince Rupert, Charles I's cousin and commander of the Royalist forces in north Wales, and offered to take custody of Harlech Castle. He was permitted to undertake that task in the following letter which was written, perhaps, after Prince Rupert had consulted his aides to establish where Harlech was:

'Lieutenant Colonell Owen,

I have taken notice of the Interest you have in the custody and Government of the Castle of Hardleigh in the County of Merioneth, and of the Imployment of Captain John Morgans [of Gelli Torwerth, Trawsfynydd] in that command under you. I shall be ready to confirme your Interest by any Commission you shall require, and to declare my allowance of Captain Morgans, and otherwise further the garrison that shall there be placed, soe as the charge of the Garrison shall excede not the benefit of it to the Cuntrey.

Soe rest
Your ffreind
Rupert.

Salop the 16th of May 1644
ffor Lieutenant Colonell Owen,
Cunstable and Governor of
Harleigh Castle, theise.'

So Rupert's permission was somewhat guarded, but the prevalent military idiocy of the time was that castles should be defended wherever possible and that, when defended, they should be attacked by opposing forces no matter what the cost in human lives and in the disruption of vital peaceful pursuits in the neighbouring areas. Yet the sprigs of the local gentry were eager for battle, as can be seen in a letter from William Wynne to his father, William Wynne of Glyn Cywarch, near Harlech, which was written at Bala on 7 February 1644:

'. . . men and Armes are expected from yo[r] parts, together with provision for 6 days march. I pray be pleased to send for the Drum from the Castle, and send it together with ye Carabine from Tanybwlch [near Maentwrog], Thus, with my duty Remembered, I remayne,

Yo.r Sonne to Comand,

William Wynne.'

The provisioning of the men referred to in this extract must have cost the district dear.

Colonel William Owen had ample time to prepare the defences of Harlech Castle. In 1646, it was attacked unsuccessfully by a Roundhead force under Colonel John Jones of Maesygarnedd and Major Moore. The Royalist defenders consisted of 16 who were named and 28 common and consequently anonymous soldiers. Apart from Colonel Owen, the following defenders were listed in a contemporary document: Sir Hugh Blaeney Kt; Mr Robert Folks (Foulkes), who died on 11 March 1647, the day after the surrender, and was burried at Llanfair on 16 March; Mr John Edwards of Chirk, 'an old man', who died in February 1647; Captain William Edwards, son of John Edwards; Lieutenant Roger Arthur; Lieutenant Roberts; John Hanmer, son of Richard Hanmer of Pentre Bant; William Edwards of Cefn-y-Wern; William Williams, 'an elderly man', who was shot in the hand about Hallowe'en and died on 19 January 1647; Meredith Lloyd of Llanfair Caereinion; Roger Burton; Francis Mason; Peter Simott; William Thomas, and Thomas Arthur, who was described as 'the Governor's man' (Colonel Owen's servant, presumably). Thus the garrison numbered 44. They were divided into two squadrons and these were each divided into three groups under the following commanders:

1st squadron	(1) William Owen and Lieutenant Arthur
	(2) Captain William Edwards and John Hanmer
	(3) Meredith Lloyd and William Edwards
2nd squadron	(1) William Williams alone
	(2) Lieutenant John Roberts and Thomas Arthur
	(3) Francis Mason and Peter Simott

The 28 soldiers were divided equally between the two squadrons and the duty of each squadron was switched around every other night. Finally, Roger Burton and William Thomas did duty on what was called the 'new wall', each taking a turn with their respective squadrons.

After a brief siege, Colonel William Owen surrendered the Castle to Major-General Mytton, on 10 March 1647. The whole garrison was required to march out of the Castle 'with their horses and Armes, proportionable to their present or past Commands, matches lighted at both ends, bullets in mouth' (as signs of surrender) to any place within four miles, as the new governor directed. There the common soldiers (there may well have been casualties among them) were to lay down their arms, except for their swords. They were then to march to Ffestiniog 'or thereabouts' by the first night and were entitled 'to stay there all night, and to have free quarters'. All were permitted to return to their homes without hindrance, provided they covered six miles a day and stayed no more than one night in any place *en route* (save in cases of sickness or other impediments). Horses were provided for all officers and gentlemen, without charge, and lastly, all the ordnance, arms and ammunition and 'provisions of warre' were to be delivered to General Mytton, for the service of Parliament, on Monday 15 March 'by tenn of the Clocke or thereabouts'.

This was the last military engagement at Harlech and the Castle was the last Royalist stronghold to fall in the first Civil War. Orders were issued later for its demolition, as indicated in a letter of Edward Wynne to a person unknown (he must have resided at no great distance from Harlech):

'Worshipfull,

I have receaved orders from the Committee at Denbigh, requiringe and authorisinge me and Edward Jones to stay all the matterialls of the Castell of Harlegh, and to see the same demolished, receaving direction from the sherife of the County, the Justices of the peace, and the rest of the gent: Therefore my request is to yow that yow would be pleased to come as far as Harlech to morrow morninge, that I have your advise herein, and to consider what is best to be done; having not els but hopeing to see you at the place and towne, but write my selfe, as alwayes I am

Your affectionate Cosen and servante
to do you both service,
Edward Wynne.

Those who have seen Aberystwyth Castle's shattered and scattered remains will appreciate how thorough the work of Parliamentary demolition could be. Perhaps Edward Wynne and Edward Jones were advised by the former's 'Cosen' merely to breach the Castle walls at certain points. Whatever was done, Harlech Castle was one of the ruins that Cromwell did not 'knock about a bit'. The massive Gate House remained largely intact and habitable in the hope perhaps, so far as the local gentry were concerned, that the justices of Great Sessions would continue to visit the town and to lodge in their accustomed if spartan quarters.

The Castle was then allowed to decay gracefully, and even the Gate House was neglected when the justices finally ceased to come after 1674. A grim reminder of their visitations, the gallows on the Morfa a little to the north of the castle rock, survived unused, for a while before they too decayed, though the town stocks for minor offenders were maintained at the instance of the Quarter Sessions in the 18th century. The Castle, honourably scarred, became the haunt of crows and a host for ivy; a useful source of dressed stone for house builders and improvers in the town; and, before dismantlement had proceeded very far, a considerable tourist attraction from the late 18th century onwards. As Crown property, it became one of the many responsibilities of HM Commissioners from the late 17th century (when the Civil List was created) until 1914, when the Ministry of Public Works assumed control. It is now administered by 'Cadw' under Welsh Office supervision. For small boys of the town the fortress became a marvellous if dangerous adventure playground, until public control was tightened.

Harlech's decline in the 17th century was certainly accelerated during the Civil War, as men were conscripted into the service of Charles I and the Royalist garrison lived off local people. In 1650, an enquiry or 'Inquest' was held into the various rights of the corporation and the jury of 16 prominent local men reported their findings on 28 May. Apart from the continuing yet ultimately futile attempt to regain or retain the Sessions, the burgesses were deeply concerned about Harlech's decline as a market town. In 1603/4, the bailiffs and burgesses had asked Sir William Maurice of Clenennau to use his influence in Parliament to have the yearly fair, held on St Andrew's Day, moved to the feast of Saints Simon and Jude because, they claimed, there was no resort of people or cattle drovers to Harlech on a day when other fairs were held in other places nearby. The jury reported in 1650:

'We say that 3 fairs are yearly kept in the town of Harleigh, and that onely a 1d. for every stallage [each market stall] used to be paid to the bailiffs, & and [sic] no tolls at all.'

The mediaeval privileges of holding fairs and markets in the borough to the exclusion of other towns or places were clearly moribund. This was bad news for Harlech as such privileges had been the very basis of its economy. By 1833, Harlech had eight annual fairs, though many of the townspeople were obliged to take their wares to distant and more flourishing centres in order to survive.

The question most commonly asked by visitors is when did the sea cease to come regularly or tidally to the foot of the castle rock, *ie:* to the Castle's Water Gate. In fact, there is no reason to believe that the sea came regularly to the rock and the Water Gate even when the castle was built. Why, then, did the castle have a Water Gate? It is likely that there was access to Harlech for vessels of fairly shallow draught along a watercourse or stream, through the marsh or saltings, which flowed more or less southwards from 'Y Gamlas' (lit. The Canal) on the Dwyryd estuary. It is known that a canal or navigation was made when Rhuddlan Castle was built, to provide access from the Dee, and it may be that nature was assisted to allow vessels to carry supplies to Harlech. Parts of such a stream may still be discerned between Tŷ Gwyn-y-Gamlas and Harlech. According to specialists on coastal formations, Morfa Harlech and Morfa Dyffryn are products of 'long-shore drift', of deposition, over extensive periods of time, of materials eroded from below these distinctive features (at Llanaber and Llandanwg respectively). References in the middle ages to the 'Harlech Marsh' and the 'Great Marsh' and to various modest drainage schemes (to the drainage of 'meers' and to 'new meadows' in 1606) tend to support this view. It is likely that, even from the outset, Harlech was supplied mainly from the Dwyryd estuary by means of a cut or canal at 'Y Gamlas' and thence along a watercourse through the saltings (which would have been exposed to attack) to the Water Gate. Harlech could not be approached by water by 1650 when the jury recorded these corporate rights:

'. . . the bailiffs of the said liberties were accustomed to have, & had [note the use of the past tense], of every ship, or other vessels, lading of any kind of grain or salt, unlading, or selling the same, at Bermouth [Barmouth], Machres [Mochres], & Gamlas, one Winchester measure, to be used in selling and venteing the said lading.'

So the Mawddach, Artro and Dwyryd estuaries once constituted Harlech's bailiwick with regard to dues imposed on imports of grain and salt. Furthermore, 'Gamlas', with its fine old house (Tŷ Gwyn-y-Gamlas), long since demolished, was sometimes referred to as 'the port of Harlech' and it continued to serve as such throughout the 19th century under the supervision of the Prichard family. Several vessels were built there. They included the snow/brig *Gomer* (161 tons), launched in 1821, which carried emigrants from Gwynedd to New York. In like manner, Mochras-Pensarn and Barmouth (Abermaw) served the people in other parts of Ardudwy.

The jury reported also on the town's rights in respect of wandering cattle, sheep and other livestock:

'. . . all waifs & estrays, within the said liberty, appertained to the said Corporation.'

In 1745, the inhabitants of Merioneth were held responsible for repairing, as they had 'always' been, the 'Harleigh Pinfold', which lay 'within the corporation town of Harleigh'. The surviving Vestry Minutes for the parish of Llandanwg (from 1788) contain many pertinent references (*ie:* when Harlech had lost its corporate status and simply formed part of the parish of Llandanwg for administrative purposes). When straying animals were placed in the pinfold or pound the owners were required to pay a fine to obtain their release.

In short, the jury of 1650 recorded the town at a low point economically, and they used the past tense consistently when referring to the rights of the corporation. Some show of corporate identity continued well into the 18th century, but this was scarcely more than an administrative reflex.

Lastly, the names of the jurors were recorded and some can be readily identified: Morys Wynne (Glyn Cywarch), John Lloyd, Humfrey Ellis, Owen Gruffyth Meiricke, Gruffith Rowland (Llanfairisaf), Edward Morys, John Owen ap Robt. Wynne, Edwarde Humffrey ap Evan, Owen Poole (Caenêst, Llanbedr), Owen ap Richard, Evan David Gruffyth, Thomas ap Humffrey and John Morgan. Those were not ordinary townsmen but local landowners and members of the gentry. They may have signed their report in order of precedence. Such men were in control of what was left of the town. The old Anglo-Norman or English families of the borough had been assimilated by intermarriage. Sion Phylip of Mochras, a noted poet and a father of poets ('Y Phylipiaid Ardudwy'), who drowned in 1620 and was buried at Llandanwg, was a descendant of Harlech's burghal families and he was not unique. The earliest parish registers of Llandanwg, which date from the 1670s, confirm that assimilation was virtually complete by the 17th century: the intended colonisers had been themselves colonised in this small and unwalled borough.

The last will and testament of Rev John Ellis, rector of Dolgellau, who died in 1665, provided for two schools for poor scholars, one at Dolgellau and the other at Harlech. They were supported by the rents of two farms in Llanaber parish. The school at Dolgellau received additional modest endowments and became known as a 'grammar school', though the classics were not taught there with any regularity. The Harlech Endowed School, which was supported by the rent of Rhuddallt Farm(about £10 per annum by the 19th century), may not have had a continuous existence from 1665. However, Rev John Ellis, a native of Llandecwyn parish to the north of Harlech, provided that a number of poor children (with preferences being given to relatives of the founder) should be taught free of charge. These free scholars were to be of one of a number of Ardudwy parishes. No school as such was ever built so scholars were taught in several places. The loft of the old Shire Hall ('Llofft yr Hall') served as a schoolroom for some time and the children were sometimes taught in the master's lodgings. Elsewhere in Ardudwy no regular schools existed until the late 18th century. Various efforts were made during the Cromwellian period, or Interregnum, and later to counter the chronic lack of educational provision in most parts of Wales but these efforts had little lasting effect. The most famous scheme was that of the 'circulating schools' of Griffith Jones of Llanddowror in the 1730s, a scheme which attracted the attention of Catherine the Great of Russia.

Camden's *Britannia*, published in 1695 reported the discovery of the gold torque in a garden near the Castle in 1692. This Celtic artifact may now be seen in the National Museum of Wales, Cardiff. Camden also reported that the district just to the north of Harlech had been visited by a strange vapour or gas (a 'prodigious fire or kindled exhalation') for a period in excess of eight months and that a brief account of it had already been published in the *Philosophical Transactions*. The story was relayed to Camden by Edward Lluyd, the keeper of the Ashmolean at Oxford and one of the most distinguished scholars of that period. Edward Lluyd's informant was Maurice Jones, who wrote from Dolgellau:

'Sir,

This letter contains no answer to your Queries about the Locusts, for I am am wholly intent at present upon giving you the best account I can, of a most dismal and prodigious accident at Harlech in this Country, the beginning of these Holy-days. It is of the unaccountable firing of sixteen Ricks of Hay, and two Barns, whereof one was full of Corn, the other of Hay. I call it unaccountable, because 'tis evident they were not burnt by common fire, but by a kindled exhalation which was often seen to come from the Sea. Of the duration whereof I cannot at present give any certain account, but am satisfied it lasted at least a fortnight or three weeks; and annoy'd the Country as well as poysoning their Grass, as firing the Hay, for the space of a mile or thereabouts. Such as have seen the fire, say 'twas a blue weak flame, easily exstinguish'd, and that it did not the least harm to any of the men who interpos'd their endeavours to save the Hay, tho' they ventur'd (perceiving it different from common fire) not only close to it, but sometimes into it. All the damage sustain'd, happen'd instantly in the night. I have enclosed a tetalogue of such as have receiv'd certain information of it; and have nothing to add, but that there are three small Tenements in the same neighbourhood (call'd Tydhin Siôn Wyn) whereof the Grass is infected, that it absolutely kill'd all manner of Cattle that feed upon it. The Grass has been infectious these three years, but not thoroughly fatal till this last. Pray send me with all convenient speed, your friends thoughts and your own of the causes, and if possible also the remedy of this surprising Phaenomenon, yrs.

Dol Gelheu, Jan. 20.

1694.

Maurice Jones supplied a list of people who had lost hay between December 24 and 29 in the previous year: 'Richard Grufydh of Lhechwedh dù [Llechwedd Du], Humfrey Owen of Garreg wen, and Richard Davidh of Erw wen, had each of them one Rick of Hay burnt . . . John Philips of Ynys Lhan Vihangel y Traethau [Ynys Llanfihangel-y-Traethau], lost one Rick of Hay — Grufydh John Owen of Kevn Trevor bâch [Cefntrefor Bach], two Ricks; and Katherine William, Widow, of Kevn Trevor Mawr, two more'; while 'Francis Evans of Glàs-vryn [Glasfryn] lost one Rick; and Richard Davidh of Erw wen, had a Barn full of Hay of three Bays building, burnt to the ground'. Edward Lluyd added that the 'fire' appeared to have come from Morfa Bychan some eight or nine miles from Harlech. He had no ready explanation to offer Maurice Jones and the anxious farmers at Harlech. He began his comments with reference to 'this surprizing and unparallel'd Meteor', but then proceeded to advance what may be called the dead locust theory, *ie:* that a swarm of locusts had settled and died and had given off a gas. Rev John Evans, who visited Harlech in 1798, over a century later, was not impressed with this. He advanced a dead herring theory. For a while at least, Harlech was much talked about in learned circles. The story lived on in the predominantly oral tradition of the district as 'y Tân Gwyllt' (the Wild Fire). For the people of the neighbourhood it was the time when something strange came from the sea near Morfa Bychan, the time when the ricks caught fire and the cattle at Tyddynsionwyn took sick and died, yet it harmed no humans.

The 18th century was truly the age of the gentry and their clerical cousins, the century of the 'Old Order' of squires and parsons in Wales as in England. Litigation rather than more or less open warfare became the usual means of settling disputes and the inbreeding of earlier times tended to give way to family alliances with their counterparts, notably in England and Ireland, formed at the marriage brokerage centres of Bath and London. The principal local gentry families in Ardudwy were the Vaughans and (after 1791) the Mostyns of Corsygedol; the Wynn(e)s, Owens, Ormsbys (of Co Sligo) and Ormsby-Gores of Glyn Cywarch; the Wynns and Nanneys of Maesyneuadd; and the Evans, Griffiths and Oakeleys of Tanybwlch. In addition, the Nanneys and Vaughans of Nannau (Hengwrt and Rûg), the county's most powerful landed family by the second half of the century, owned lands in and around Harlech and involved themselves in the town's affairs. The lesser or petty gentry were also quite well represented and some shaded off into the lesser freeholders who were more numerous in Ardudwy than in any other part of Merioneth, in spite of the existence of the large estates, a fact confirmed by the electoral lists of freeholders of the county. The grand gentry's power was essentially economic, for they possessed well-nucleated and extensive estates, but it was expressed in social and political terms. The Vaughan family of Corsygedol dominated the political stage from 1701 to 1791. They provided, with the fairly ready connivance of their relatives in other parts of the county, Merioneth's MPs for all but eight of those years: Richard Vaughan (1665/6-1734), 1701-1734; William Vaughan (1707-1775), son of Richard Vaughan, 1734-1768; and Evan Lloyd Vaughan (1709/10-1791), brother of William Vaughan, 1774-1791. The gap between 1768 and 1774 was due to Evan Lloyd Vaughan's refusal of the seat in the former year but he accepted nomination (election) in 1774. Few elections were contested in Merioneth until the second third of the 19th century. Evan Lloyd Vaughan, the last of the male line, was succeeded by Sir Robert Williames Vaughan of Nannau, Bart (1768-1843), who retired in 1836. The grand gentry took their turns in such offices as High Sheriff of Merioneth and Evan Lloyd Vaughan of Corsygedol was Constable/Mayor of Harlech from 1754 to 1791, though neither of the twin offices had any real significance. The gentry and their clerical cousins also controlled the county administration as magistrates through the Quarter Sessions. Between them and the poor (landless labourers, paupers and the like) lay the 'middling sort of people', from those who practised medicine and law to those who plied their crafts in small damp cottages. Some prospered due to a mixture of good fortune, sound health, business acumen, sharp practice and genuine ability, but the ascendancy of the gentry survived well into the 19th century. A local middle class emerged quite steadily in the course of the 18th century. An examination of scores of local wills and inventories of goods (personal estate) for the 18th century discloses that £1,000 worth of personal property was a rare fortune in Ardudwy, where the stock, household goods and other effects of relatively prosperous tenant farmers seldom exceeded £100 to £200. The overland cattle trade (to England) and maritime trade were the main sources of such capital as existed. There was, in fact, a marked expansion of maritime trade in Ardudwy during the closing decades of the century, and local shipbuilding (at Barmouth, Mochras and on the Dwyryd) reflected this increase. The small port of Barmouth was dredged, deepened and enlarged under a private Harbour Improvement Act between 1797 and 1802, and local mariners began to engage in the slate trade of Gwynedd as it showed promise towards the end of the century. The outbreak of war with France in 1793 disrupted maritime trade and led to a bread famine in the district for several years. Infant mortality rates were high during the 1790s. However, a century of relative peace and stability brought new levels of prosperity to the gentry and to families of the emergent middle class in Ardudwy. This was reflected in extensions to existing mansions (*eg:* Corsygedol), in the building of new and larger farm and other houses, and in the introduction of improved farming methods. The poor relied on parish relief and alms, the main form of which was 'cardod' — flour, potatoes and suchlike — dispensed at various times but notably on St Thomas's Day, just three days before Christmas. Life was hard and insecure for all but a few and Ardudwy was, in this respect, a microcosm of Wales in the 18th century.

While the gentry dominated, they were certainly mindful of their obligations. Their retainers and tenants accorded them a kind of tribal loyalty and they, in turn, ensured that alms and patronage were dispensed. They prided themselves on their ancient British lineage and some were lavish in their hospitality. Some were even given to excess. When Thomas Pennant passed the mansion of Tanybwlch near Maentwrog in 1773 he noted that successive heads of the Evans family had drunk themselves into early graves, and the parish registers support his view. Some of the lesser gentry ruined themselves and their families in a vain attempt to keep up with their more successful cousins, though others added to their modest incomes from land by engaging in the professions. In general, Ardudwy's gentry were Tories of the 'constitutional' sort, and traditionalists, but they became increasingly anglicised in the course of the 18th century. This adoption of English speech and manners formed one kind of division in an outwardly organic society, and this was steadily emphasised, towards the end of the century, by the spread of Nonconformity among the middle layers of society — among some of the lesser gentry, the freeholders, tenant farmers, some of the tradespeople, most of the craftsmen and others. The grand gentry tried to quell this spring tide but it proved irresistible. Calvinistic Methodism spread throughout the district and the Baptists established themselves, along with the Calvinistic Methodists, at Harlech and in other northerly parts of Ardudwy. These sectarian differences often reflected individual and family influences. Even in the late 18th century the Nonconformists exerted a sobering influence upon traditional society. Interludes performed by travelling players, folk songs and dances, and other aspects of the older society were frowned upon, and began to disappear, but the process was a gradual one, and some of the former fitful gaiety survived into the 19th century, sustained in part within the inns and taverns, and by regular visitations of Welsh gypsies among whom were members of Abraham (Abram) Wood's extensive family and, perhaps, Abraham Wood himself as self-styled 'King of the Welsh Gypsies'. He was buried in Llangelynin churchyard, south of the river Mawddach, at the beginning of the new century, when over 100 years old.

In Ardudwy, the 18th century was, therefore, a century of stability and relative prosperity, under the firm but sometimes genial ascendancy of the grand gentry and their clerical cousins. However, it was also a century of accelerating economic, social and religious change, the effects of which were to be more clearly experienced and discerned during the 19th century.

By the early 18th century, Harlech was a thoroughly Welsh town, whose poor inhabitants sought to gain a living from their rocky acres and partially drained marshlands. The pastoralists, mostly tenants of the major local estates or of lesser landlords, produced cattle and sheep which supported such crafts as skinning, tanning, saddlery, shoemaking, gloving, weaving and knitting, hatmaking, tailoring and millinery. Drovers were also prominent in this largely pastoral economy, and they acted, to some extent, as general business or commission agents for the farmers, both freeholders and tenants, and for the gentry. Seafaring became an additional occupation. The inhabitants can be readily traced in the parish registers of Llandanwg and the neighbouring parishes of Llanfihangel-y-Traethau and Llanfair. Two bailiffs of Harlech, as representatives of the burgesses, still attended the Merioneth Quarter Sessions, but the town's borough status was already spectral. The bailiffs were commonly tradesmen and other ordinary inhabitants of the town. They included, in 1750, Evan Anwyl of the Red Lion, Harlech, innkeeper, who died in 1759 when his personal estate was valued at just over £137. As a member of the Anwyl family of Panteinion in south Merioneth, Evan Anwyl could claim descent from Gruffydd ap Cynan, a Dublin-born King of Gwynedd, yet his personal estate in 1759, as one of the town's leading inhabitants, says much for the general poverty of Harlech. Some of his descendants, however, were to prosper at Harlech, Barmouth and Dolgellau during the 19th century. Harlech contained no members of the legal or medical professions in the 18th century. Lawyers (attorneys) and surgeons existed in the district but they did not choose to live in Harlech.

Some idea of the town's condition in 1706 can be gained from a letter written by Rev Ellis Wynne (Elis Wyn) of Lasynys (1670/1-1734) to his kinswoman Margaret Owen of Brogyntyn (Porkington) and Glyn Cywarch. Ellis Wynne was then rector of Llandanwg parish. When he received news that Margaret Owen intended to visit Glyn Cywarch, clearly a rare event, he wrote to her in the hope that she would provide money for a church at Harlech. He was concerned about the spiritual laxity of the inhabitants who were, he claimed, reluctant to attend their sea-washed and often sand-filled parish church at Llandanwg. He begged Margaret Owen to provide a church at Harlech and suggested that the ancient and ruined Shire Hall (and Town Hall) in the town might be renovated to serve that end (though, strictly, the building was not in Margaret Owen's grant, since it belonged to the town and corporation of Harlech — but the gentry did not trouble themselves with such legal quibbles):

'My Parishioners of Llandanwg & my self are extreamly desirous of a chappell again st Harlech which wou'd be an unspeakable benefit, comfort & conveniency not only to ye Town but also to ye whole [parish] except 3 houses only [*ie:* in the vicinity of the parish church] & those ly [lie] as near to another Church yt [that] is just at hand [at Llanfair].'

He noted that Harlech had formerly possessed three chapels — the Constable's chapel, the garrison chapel in the Castle, and the burgesses's chapel dedicated to Mary Magdalen nearby

— but these were deemed unsuitable for various reasons. He noted that the Magdalen Chapel 'is now not only demolish'd but the stones of it quite carry'd away into other buildings in the Town long ago' (Ty'r Eiddew or Ivy Cottage now occupies the site) and he continued:
'. . . notwithstanding ye ready benevolence of some persons of worth and ability, yet our own pt.cular poverty, the scarcity of money & of stones [no comment!] at hand is such that we must needs desist from this good enterprize, unless we have ye advantage of some other old building to help us: and that we can nowhere espy unless yo.r ladp [ladyship] & Mr. William Owen out of yo.r bounteous & pious disposition will be pleased to bestow upon us the Old Shire Hall to this purpose, which tho almost ruin'd yet would save us a considerable part of the expence, for which it might not only supply us with stones but also save a building perhaps in some parts of it which peradventure might suffice as they are.'
Perhaps Margaret Owen was not in a giving mood, for the Shire Hall was not greatly altered until it was incorporated into the new Castle Hotel in 1876. Ellis Wynne seems to have lost interest after his translation from Llandanwg to Llanfair in 1711. He continued to live at Lasynys, to the north of Harlech, where he added a wing to the interesting old house. He is celebrated as the author of *Gweledigaethau y Bardd Cwsg* (Visions of the Sleeping Bard) and, perhaps, as the finest writer of Welsh prose. The Anglicans of Harlech had to wait until 1840 for a church to be built in their town. Meanwhile, the Calvinistic Methodists became active and built their first chapel (*Moreia*) in 1769. The Baptists came a few years later and they built their first chapel (*Bethel*), on the edge of the castle green, in 1786. Capel Bethel was built on land owned by Robert Humphreys (1765-1840) of Llanfairuchaf, near Llanfair, one of the founders of the sect in Harlech. It became known as 'Capel-y-Dwfr' (the Water Chapel) and, while the chapel has long since been demolished, the small cemetery, (which contains the remains, *inter alia*, of my great-great-great-grandfather, Evan Lloyd (1776-1847) of Cilcychwyn) survives to this day. Early baptisms were performed in the former mill pond near the castle (Llyn-y-Felin). The inhabitants of Harlech were steadily converted from Anglicanism to Nonconformity in the late 18th and early 19th centuries.

In about 1730 Ellis Rowland of Harlech, poet, died when around 80 years of age. His patrons included certain local families, and among his surviving works are elegies to Samuel Poole of Tyddyn-y-Felin and Edward Lloyd of Cwm Bychan (who died in 1728), both of Llanfair parish. By this time the gentry had largely withdrawn their patronage of local poets, and freeholders like Edward Lloyd were unable to assume this role in any effective or continuing way. Edward Lloyd had a life estate ('in fee tail male') in the rocky acres of Cwm Bychan, a secluded upland valley, and at his death his personal estate was valued at just over £154. Thomas Pennant visited Cwm Bychan in 1773 where he was entertained in true 'ancient British style' by Evan Lloyd (d1785), son of Edward Lloyd, who produced his pedigree back to Bleddyn ap Cynfyn, Prince of north Wales and Powys (d1075).

From Cwm Bychan, in 1773, Thomas Pennant and his riding companion, Rev John Lloyd (1733-1793), who was a first cousin of Evan Lloyd, descended into Harlech:
'From Cwm Bychan, took the road to Harlech, a small and very poor town, remarkable only for its castle, which is seated on a lofty rock, facing the Irish sea, above an extensive marsh, once occupied by the water . . .'
This brief description appeared in the first volume of Pennant's *Tours in Wales* published in 1778. In fact, Thomas Pennant was the forerunner of many literary tourists to visit Harlech in the late 18th century, and many artists painted the Castle and the surroundings about this time and later. They included the Cotman brothers, John Varley and the great Turner. The Napoleonic Wars (1793-1815) encouraged such tours of Wales as did the Romantic Movement, with its preoccupation with ancient ruins, mountains, torrents, cataracts and nature in its wilder moods. Ardudwy could not be bettered.

This was a period of feverish enthusiasms, a time of strange cults which were given local expression in the person of 'Mari y Fantell Wen' (Mary of the White Robe) and her followers. Mari, or Mary Evans, came to this district from Anglesey in 1780. She claimed to be the bride of Christ and, on Sundays, she and her followers donned white robes for their meetings in the hills. Her following increased considerably in the area between Ffestiniog and Harlech but, though Mari claimed that she would never die, she went to her reward in Talsarnau and her mortal remains were buried at Llanfihangel churchyard on 28 October 1789. By then, Nonconformity was beginning to restrain the wilder excesses of this kind of enthusiasm, and many of Mari's followers probably became pillars of their chapels, their white robes returned to the use for which they were intended, *ie:* bed linen.

The Vestry minutes of Llandanwg parish (from 1788) indicate that the men of Harlech had no great enthusiasm for the war with revolutionary France. They were obliged to contribute towards the Merioneth Militia in which the gentry took such delight, but they preferred to pay money for the services of others. For example, an account of 22 May 1797 reads: 'paid to the Militia man Llandecwyn [£] 1-13-0 Sarvant Maesyneuadd'. David Owen served in the Militia since payments were recorded in 1792 (£3) — 'to Dav^{d} Owen Malitiaman' and in 1797-8 (£2) — 'paid David Owen Militia man'. In 1794-5, Llewelyn Ellis of Harlech was paid 3s 6d 'towards a man to serve in the Navy' and 6s 9d for a journey to Pwllheli 'to seek a man'. He was also paid 2s 6d for a journey to 'Cricketh on the same account'. From this and other evidence it seems safe to conclude that the men of Harlech were not exactly fired with martial ardour. Yet several local mariners encountered Breton and French Privateers in the Western Approaches and the English Channel. The Irish Sea was relatively safe, and this was in sharp contrast to the somewhat earlier American War of Independence (1775-1783) when many vessels were captured, and John Paul Jones sailed on the *Ranger* to Whitehaven, Cumbria, where he sacked the town in which he had once lived. Some local mariners were captured during the Napoleonic Wars and were imprisoned in Breton and French gaols. For example, the sloop *Harlech Castle*, commanded by Captain William Jones (1765-1838) of Cefntrefor Fawr (and later of the Ship Aground in Talsarnau), was captured in 1795 by a French frigate; master and crew were imprisoned at Arras. William Jones and his men soon escaped. They crossed the Channel on a stolen craft and landed on the Kent coast where they were greeted, in Welsh, by members of the Flintshire Militia, who were stationed there to ward off possible invasion.

In spite of the growing influence of Nonconformity throughout the district the Old Order of squire and parson retained an air of permanence in this locality at the close of the 18th century.

TO BE SOLD BY AUCTION,

(WITHOUT RESERVE)

At the house of Mr. John Prichard, at Ty-gwyn y-Gamllas, in the county of Merioneth, on Friday the 10th day of September, 1819, at two o'clock in the afternoon :—

THE FRAME of a NEW BRIG, partly built, and on the stocks, in a convenient building yard, at Ty gwyn-y-Gamllas, on the border of Traeth-bach, in the county of Merioneth, with all the Timber, Planks, Stove, and other materials, provided towards completing the same.

The keel is 63 feet in length, and it is supposed the vessel will carry 200 tons or upwards.

The ground timbers are all placed and copper-fastened.

For further particulars, apply to Mr. ELLIS. WILLIAMS, Maentwrog, or Mr. JOHN LLOYD, Solicitor, Pen y Glanne, Maentwrog, Merionethshire.

ABOVE: Maesygarnedd in Cwm Nantcol, home of Col. John Jones. The house dates from c1580. LEFT: Colonel John Jones of Maesygarnedd, regicide, with a facsimile signature from the Death Warrant of Charles I, 1649. (NLW) RIGHT: An example of shipbuilding at Tŷ Gwyn in the early 19th century. The vessel was the brig *Gomer* launched in 1821. (GAS)

ABOVE: Tŷ Gwyn-y-Gamlas to the north of Harlech. The house appears to date from the late 16th century. The warehouse is a later structure. Damaged in the great flood of 1927 the stones of the house were used to fill a breach in the sea wall. BELOW: 'Tegwin' (Tŷ Gwyn), the 'Port of Harlech', from a painting by John Varley, 1827. (Both MU)

Grand Junction Wharf
Brentford Decr 30th 1826

Mr John Jones

Sir

Annex'd I beg to hand you an Invoice of Grain agreeably to your Order dated the first of November. The Grain is Ship'd by the Gomer Captn Richard Pritchard who Sailed last Wednesday Week, and of which I presume you have been inform'd by his Letter to his Wife. I could not send the Grain by the Bardsey, as she was quite full. I have had your Grain Insured, which I presume you will approve of, as We have had of late some very boisterous [illegible] and the Rate of Insurance is low— As I have

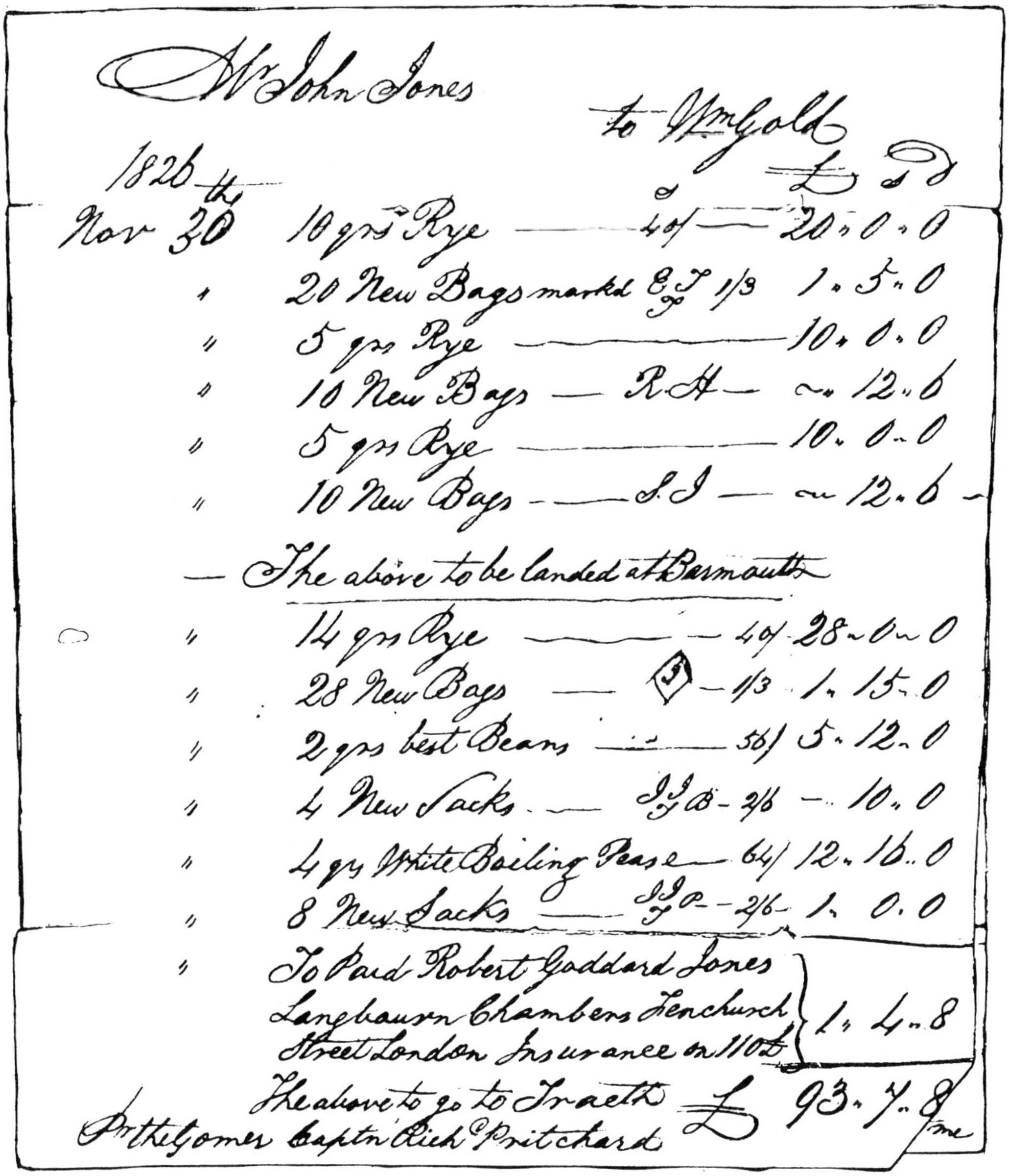

Mr John Jones

to Wm Gold

1826		£ s d
Nov 30th	10 qrs Rye — 40/ —	20.0.0
"	20 New Bags marked E J 1/3	1.5.0
"	5 qrs Rye —	10.0.0
"	10 New Bags — R.H —	–.12.6
"	5 qrs Rye —	10.0.0
"	10 New Bags — S.J —	–.12.6
	— The above to be landed at Barmouth	
"	14 qrs Rye — 40/	28.0.0
"	28 New Bags — [3] — 1/3	1.15.0
"	2 qrs best Beans — 56/	5.12.0
"	4 New Sacks — J J B - 2/6	–.10.0
"	4 qrs White Boiling Pease — 64/	12.16.0
"	8 New Sacks — J J P — 2/6	1.0.0
"	To Paid Robert Goddard Jones Langbourn Chambers Fenchurch Street London Insurance on 110£	1.4.8

The above to go to Traeth £ 93.7.8

Pr the Gomer Captn Richd Pritchard Jme

OPPOSITE ABOVE: The brig *Gomer* (161 tons), launched in 1821, carried emigrants from Gwynedd to New York in the 1820s and 1830s. BELOW: Part of the letter of 1826 from William Gold to John Jones. ABOVE: The invoice which accompanied the letter of 1826. The money was conveyed to William Gold a year later by John Owen, a cattle drover. (All GAS)

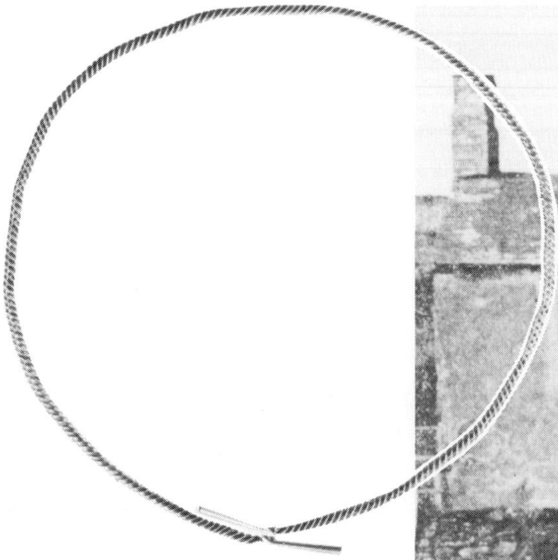

LEFT: The gold torque discovered at Harlech in 1692. (By Permission of the National Museum of Wales, Cardiff.) RIGHT: Lasynys Fawr, the home of Ellis Wynne on Morfa Harlech. He added the wing on the left. BELOW: Glyn Cywarch mansion near Talsarnau dates from the early Stuart period. (NLW) OPPOSITE ABOVE: The title page of the (left) first and (right) second editions of Ellis Wynne's masterpiece, 1703 and 1728. (NLW) BELOW: Part of the Rev Ellis Wynne's letter to Margaret Owen of Glyn Cywarch, 1706, with the writer's most elaborate signature. (NLW)

GWELEDIGAETHEU

Y

Bardd Cwsc.

Y

RHANN GYNTAF.

Argraphwyd yn *Llundain* gan E. *Powell*, i'r Awdwr. 1703.

GWELEDIGAETHEU

Y

Bardd Cwsc.

Y

RHANN CYNTAF.

Argraphwyd yn y Flwyddyn 1728

'Tis so far from that, that it will be an effectuall means to derive upon ye same a Blessing of Continuation & Increase, as it woud be a good step towards reviving here the neglected Worship of Almighty God & promoting ye Salvation of Souls many whereof as it will be always) canot & many will not go to ye other Church but very seldom, some once a year & some far seldomer than so.

Most heartily begging You woud excuse & favorably answer this well-intended Request, & accept of my weak unfeigned prayrs for the Prosperity & Happiness of yr Self & hopefull Posterity I conclude at last,

Dear Madam, Yr Ladyships most humbly devoted Servt whilest [illegible]

Lâs Ynys
Novbr 9th 1706.

ABOVE: A highly romantic view of the Castle and its setting by C. Childs from a sketch by G. Pickering. BELOW: Another romantic depiction of the Castle, unsigned. (Both NLW)

The Most Wretched Place

Such was the miserable state of the town at this time that many tourists, who published their impressions, simply passed through after visiting the Castle. J. Hucks, when on a pedestrian tour of north Wales in 1794, arrived at Harlech one evening and sought to enter the Castle with these results:

'. . . some of the inhabitants observing our operations, and probably taking us for free-booters, gave the alarm; and mustering a formidable body of forces, marched in military array, to dispossess us of our stronghold. But we soon pacified our opponents, and having convinced them that our intentions were neither predatory nor hostile, they retired to an ale-house to banish sorrow, and indulge themselves, at our expence, in copious libations of ale.'

The 'ale-house' was probably the Red Lion Inn a tenement of the Corsygedol estate, just beyond the eastern edge of the castle green, which was then kept by Watkin Anwyl (1739-1823) and his wife Catherine (Jones) (1736-1821). It was then the town's main hostelry but, while the Corsygedol Arms Inn at Barmouth was rebuilt in 1795, the Red Lion at Harlech received no such attention. Its inadequacies were tellingly described by Rev John Evans, one of the most informative literary tourists of this period, in 1798:

'It was now near evening, and prudence invited us to make this cheerless spot our residence for the night; but the inn offered no bed, nor anything better than a dirt floor, strewed with a few rushes. The chilling idea determined us to proceed to encounter difficulties . . .'

These tourists quitted Harlech and proceeded northwards to Tanybwlch. According to Evans, the Red Lion was in keeping with the wretchedness of the town:

'We were surprised to find the county town of Merioneth a few miserable cottages on the top of a bare rock . . . in its present state it is the most wretched place I ever saw. Though it is the county town, there is no vestige of a public building, unless four roofless walls, like a barn, that has undergone the ordeal of fire, can be termed one. This however is the county guild, and here, at the last election, Sir Robert Vaughan (of Nannau) was chaired as Knight of the Shire.'

Evans and his companions required a guide for their journey to Tanybwlch and here they were fortunate to encounter John Richards (1751-1826) of Tŷ Mawr, a skinner and glover, who soon became the regular guide at Harlech:

'While inquiring for a guide, we observed a decent looking man at a cottage door, directly opposite . . .; he ingenuously owned the guide was absent, but as he understood every inch of the ground, he would, if we pleased, conduct us safe to our destination. An air of frankness visible in his countenance, and a fluency in speaking English, (very unusual here) prejudiced us in his favour, and we instantly closed with his proposal; and to his credit, let it be recorded, we found in him a faithful and intelligent guide . . .'

Rev Richard Warner, who passed through Harlech in 1798-9, also employed John Richards. Having crossed from Penmorfa in Caernarfonshire in 'a small leaky skiff' (the ferry), Warner made his way over the Morfa to the town in showery weather:

'Another heavy shower sent us drenched into the town of Harlech, and obliged us to have recourse to a bottle of brandy which we found here in great perfection [it may well have been smuggled]. A civil, attentive creature, John Richards (the guide to Cwm Bychan, the lakes, &c. whom I cannot help recommending — on account of his superior sagacity, as well as civility) offered us his services to conduct us to the Castle, and was accepted as our escort . . .). Every external circumstance induced us to continue at Harlech; the wind blew an hurricane, the rain fell in torrents, and the evening was setting in . . . But unfortunately no beds were to be procured in the place, and we were reduced to braving the storm, or sleeping on the floor . . . we quickly resolved to disregard the weather and proceed to Barmouth. Fortifying ourselves, therefore, with a little more of the landlady's neat Coniac [sic], we sallied forth to meet the rage of the elements . . .'

The landlady referred to was probably Mrs Catherine Anwyl. The landlord of the Red Lion, like most local innkeepers in this period, was a farmer, so that the inn would have been commonly left in his wife's charge (in fact, many inns and taverns were kept by women, usually widows, at this time in Gwynedd and later).

John Richards was certainly one of Harlech's leading inhabitants. In 1776, he had married Elizabeth Anwyl (1747-1835), a daughter of Evan Anwyl (1702-1759) of Tŷ Mawr (a bailiff of Harlech in 1750), so John Richards, skinner and glover, was a brother-in-law of Watkin Anwyl. A well used *English Grammar* bears his signature and the date 1786: his fluency in English was clearly exceptional at the time. When Watkin Anwyl died in 1823, his personal estate (he had no real property) was valued at £97 10s. The condition of Harlech's poor is difficult to imagine. It can be said that the daughters of Evan Anwyl, Watkin's father, 'married well' since, apart from Elizabeth, Catherine married Charles Blair, a shopkeeper of St Chadd's parish, Salop, in 1756; Jane married Solomon Griffiths, a customs officer, in 1764; and Mary married Captain Meyrick Ellis (1744-1807), a master mariner, in 1775. This was, in fact, a successful commercial family in the making. Watkin Anwyl's son Evan Anwyl (1768-1849) was master and part-owner of the sloop *William and Nancy* of Barmouth (a vessel built at Mochras in 1785) in 1786 and his father was a shareholder in the venture ('Harddlech' was the form used in the Beaumaris Shipping Register). The younger Evan Anwyl retired from the sea to become a grocer in Harlech and master of the Endowed School in the 1820s. His sons Watkin (1792-1876) and David (1795-1876) were to become leading merchants at Dolgellau and Barmouth respectively; they also invested in local shipping. This combination of farming, innkeeping, shopkeeping, various trades and seafaring was typical of the emergent middle class in Ardudwy from the late 18th century onwards. The professions of law and medicine often followed commercial success.

A third clerical tourist, Rev Walter Bingley, published these impressions of his visit to Harlech in 1798:

'Once the principal town in Merionethshire, it is now dwindled into an insignificant village, containing not more than four or five hundred inhabitants . . . the houses and castle are built on a cliff that immediately overhangs the marsh. Not far from the castle there is a small building, once the town-hall, now a school-room, in which, however, the member of parliament for the county is still elected . . .'

Such well-heeled tourists were clearly amazed at the condition of the town and the ancient Shire/Town Hall. Sadly, the condition of the inhabitants attracted scant attention.

Finally, the comments of Richard Fenton, a rather caustic barrister from Pembrokeshire, who visited Harlech in 1808, deserve recital:

'The town, or rather poor village of Harlech, is the most forlorn, beggarly place imaginable, yet it boasts to be the County Town, and here the Member is returned. The building they show you for the Town Hall is now ruinous and unroofed, and yet within these walls the Member is returned. It had been a small though respectable building, having two opposite doors cased with cut stone arched [sic], and a moulding of Freestone running along the wall to the East, where was the chief magistrate's [*ie:* the mayor's] Seat. Their Charter, if they ever had one, has been lost, yet they were used to make Burgesses, that privilege, on what authority I know not, having been exercised conjointly by the families of Corsygedol and Maesyneuadd, Houses tracing their origin to the same Head. There has been a Chapel and a place of Interment opposite to the Castle, as the man told me [John Richards]. He had taken the site to make tanpits of, and in digging them, he fell on several Skeletons, without anything like a covering of Wood or Stone, in a bed of marl. There was a Skeleton of a woman far advanced in her pregnancy, as there were small ribs mixed with the larger, and a small skull. At the upper end of the Town, the end towards Barmouth, there appears a large old house, as if there had formerly been some consequence attached to it . . .'

This final reference to the remains of 'a large old house' is of particular interest. It was probably the shell of a mediaeval town house (of the Nannau or Hengwrt families) called 'Plas yn Harlech' (*Plas* — mansion). It was later rebuilt to the order of Sir Robert W. Vaughan Bart MP, to become the Blue Lion Inn.

These impressions confirm the miserable condition of Harlech during the Napoleonic Wars and there were more reverses to come. By an Enclosure Act of 1806 (46 Geo III), Morfa Harlech (within the parishes of Llandanwg and Llanfihangel-y-Traethau), or a substantial part of it, and substantial acreages of the uplands, were enclosed at the instance (and expense) of the principal landowners, the gentry of Corsygedol, Glyn Cywarch, Maesyneuadd, Tanybwlch and Nannau-Hengwrt. On certain conditions, they received the lion's share of the Morfa and upland allotments which had previously been the property of the 'town and liberty'. Other Morfa allotments went to lesser freeholders and some were purchased at public auctions held at the Red Lion, Harlech, in 1807. Poor cottagers who depended upon common grazing rights were generally excluded. Large acreages of sheepwalks which, in some cases, proved to be valuable slate-bearing lands, were similarly enclosed (hence the miles of mountain walls in the district) and disposed of. Morfa Dyffryn was virtually incorporated into the Corsygedol estate. To those who had much more was given, and to those who had little even that was taken from them — this was the principle of the 'Enclosure Movement' in Wales as in England. With the enclosure of as yet unappropriated parts of Morfa Harlech the burgesses lost their lordship. Richard Fenton made these slighting comments in 1808:

'About two years ago, an Act passed for inclosing a Common called Harlech Marsh, on which were bred famous Ponies, and now it appears divided into good sized fields, separated by Fences at right Angles, and is getting into fine cultivation very fast. The beggarly burgesses of Harlech, who had a right of common here [more than that acording to the fee-farm grant of 1316], represented it as a great Lordship. It may be a loss to a beggarly individual, but it must form a great accession to the wealth of the Country.'

It must be admitted that the main beneficiaries, the gentry, through their stewards, undertook to drain the Morfa and they distributed their lowland and upland allotments among their tenants (several upland farms gained detached fields on the Morfa). Some wholly new farms were created on Morfa Harlech by the stewards of Corsygedol and Glyn Cywarch. The Morfa was later drained by experts imported from East Anglia and the now familiar patchwork pattern of fields began to take shape, though many fields, it seems, resulted from much earlier enclosures called locally 'Pumrhydau' (*Pumrhwd* = five square roods or an acre and a quarter) and 'Corsydd' (*Cors* = marshland or former marshy ground). Gorse was introduced to the area as a hedging plant at this time. However, no matter what 'improvements' ensued, the townsmen of Harlech were dismayed by the loss of their ancient grazing rights below the town to the all-powerful though largely absentee gentry, but they were obliged to accept the situation.

The large estates were greatly extended as the Tithe Commutation Returns of 1839-40 indicate. By 1840, Corsygedol comprised 15,000 acres, Glyn Cywarch over 8,000 and Nannau, Hengwrt and Rûg some 24,000 acres (the first two in Ardudwy and the third, composite estate, in Merioneth).

Some of the Nannau-Hengwrt allotments on Morfa Harlech became the site of a race course ('Cwrs Rasus'). The well-marked circuit has since been obscured by conifers, but the once celebrated Harlech Hunt and Races were founded by Lieutenant-Colonel Griffith ap Howel Vaughan, commandant of the Royal Merioneth Militia, who succeeded his brother as Constable (and Mayor) of Harlech in 1807 (these twin offices then seemed firmly lodged in the Vaughan family of Hengwrt and Nannau). The first day of each annual meeting was usually devoted to hare coursing with the hounds of Ynysfor, and the second day consisted of horse and pony races. These meetings were generally held in November before the gentry left for London. A large window was installed at 'Tŷ Rasus' (Races House) to serve as a grandstand, *ie:* where the grand stood. These meetings were commonly reported in the *Carnarvon and Denbigh Herald* during the 1840s and 1850s. After each day's meeting, the gentry and their associates met for food, wine and merriment in the Blue Lion at Harlech (following the opening of the new inn in about 1830). The Harlech Hunt and Races continued in spite of the death of Sir R. W. Vaughan in 1843 and that of his brother, Colonel Vaughan, the founder, in 1847, but patronage declined quite steadily in the 1850s. The race course was otherwise used by tenant farmers for grazing and other purposes.

The enclosures of 1806 deprived the town of its remaining landed patrimony and, in 1835, the Municipal Corporations Act denied Harlech an elected town council in place of the burgesses and bailiffs under the Charter of 1284. In January 1836, spirited elections were held in the boroughs of Gwynedd, such as Pwllheli and Caernarfon, where Reform candidates were generally victorious, in spite of the machinations of the gentry who had formerly controlled the boroughs through nominees or placemen as burgesses and, more important, as bailiffs. There was to be no election at Harlech, since the Act of 1835 simply passed over the smaller boroughs. This was not surprising in Harlech's case, but it did mean that, by default, the town formally lost the last vestiges of its borough status, and became part of the parish of Llandanwg for all local administrative purposes: some 550 years of precarious borough status thus ended in 1835.

All that remained to Harlech of its former county status was the nomination of candidates and the proclamation of members for the shire in the county parliamentary elections.

ABOVE: An amusing sketch of the entrance to the Castle with figures, unsigned. (GAS) BELOW: The Castle from Penllech by W. Wallis after H. Gastineau illuminated by morning sunlight. (NLW)

ABOVE: The Castle, Morfa Harlech (newly enclosed) and the Blue Lion Inn (right) by F. Jones after F. Dimes, Day & Co Lithograph. BELOW: This picture by Baynes, del W. Woolnoth, sculp, 1824, is most notable for the distinct stream at the base of the rock. (Both NLW)

County of MERIONETH, to wit. } **Be it Remembered** that on the Sixteenth Day of September in the fifty eighth Year of the Reign of our Sovereign Lord GEORGE the third —— by the Grace of GOD of the United Kingdom of Great Britain and Ireland KING, Defender of the Faith, Watkin Anwyl — of Harlech in the said County, Innkeeper, and Owen Davies of Harlech aforesaid Innholder personally came before us Griffith Owen and Richard Hughes Clerks two of His Majesty's Justices of the Peace in and for the said County, and acknowledged themselves to owe to our said Lord the King, that is to say, the said Watkin Anwyl —— the Sum of TEN Pounds, and the said Owen Davies the — Sum of Ten Pounds, of lawful Money of Great Britain, to be made and levied of their Goods and Chattels, Lands and Tenements respectively, to the use of our said Lord the King, his Heirs and Successors, if the said Watkin Anwyl shall make Default in the Condition under-written.

The Condition of this Recognizance is such, THAT WHEREAS the above-bounden Watkin Anwyl — — — — — — — — is authorized and impowered to keep a Common Inn, Ale-house, or Victualling-house, for ONE YEAR from the TWENTY-NINTH Day of this present Month of SEPTEMBER, in the House where he now dwelleth at Harlech — — aforesaid; Therefore if he the said Watkin Anwyl shall keep and maintain good Order and Rule, and shall suffer no Disorders or unlawful Games in his said House, nor in any Out-house, Yard, Garden, or Premises, during the said Term; THEN this Recognizance shall be void, or else remain in its force.

TAKEN and acknowledged the Day and Year first above written, before us, Griffith Owen, Richd. Hughes

Merionethshire Timber.

TT BE SOLD BY AUCTION,

At the house of Watkin Anwyl, in Harlech, on Friday, the 5th day of November, 1813, between the hours of 3 and 7 o'clock in the afternoon, subject to conditions then to be produced:—

Lot I—160 Oak Timber Trees.
2—208 Ditto
3—204 Ditto
4—190 Ditto
5—162 Ditto
6—242 Ditto

Also several Lots of Cordwood.

The above Timber is well worth the attention of House and Ship-builders, and lies on Glynn Demesne, in the parish of Llanfihangel y Traethau, within a mile of the navigable river, called Traeth bach.

For further particulars, apply to FRANCIS ELLIS, at Glynn.

ABOVE: The former Red Lion Inn at Penllech, now an undertaker's workshop. (MW) LEFT: Recognizance of Watkin Anwyl, landlord of the Red Lion, dated 16 September 58 Geo III. (GAS) RIGHT: Notice of a timber sale at the Red Lion in 1813 from the *North Wales Gazette.* (UCNWA)

LEFT: The former Blue Lion Inn c1830, now Plas Café. (MW) BELOW: The town and castle as depicted by J.M.W. Turner c1834. (NLW) RIGHT: Sir Robert Williames Vaughan (1768-1843) of Nannau, Bart MP, Harlech's chief patron from c1830 until his death. (GAS)

The Age of Renewal

During the 19th century the ordinary people of Harlech and its environs continued to make what they could of their poor town. The economy of Gwynedd was transformed with the expansion of the slate industry and the associated maritime trade and, although Harlech was at some distance from the nearest major centre of the slate industry Blaenau Ffestiniog and its maritime outlet, Porthmadog, where the new harbour was opened in 1825 and linked by tramway to Ffestiniog in 1836, the slate industry and the maritime slate trade provided work for men and boys of Harlech as quarry labourers, quarrymen (or 'quarriers'), slate loaders, mariners and so on at Ffestiniog and Porthmadog. Local farmers and even farm workers derived some benefit too. Farmers profited from the increased demand for their produce at Ffestiniog and related growth centres, while male farm workers were sometimes able to secure higher wages due to increased competition for labour in the slate industry. Various agricultural improvements ensued. Many of these were sponsored by the county agricultural society, such as improved animal husbandry and more effective land drainage. Ploughing matches became a regular feature of local rural life from the 1840s. Communications, hitherto notoriously bad, were greatly improved by the creation of local turnpike trusts in 1833, regular coach services between Caernarfon and Barmouth *via* Harlech from the same year, and by the completion of the coast railway in 1867. Tourism became an increasingly important component of the district's and the town's economy, and facilities for visitors were steadily improved. The railway link had momentous consequences for the town; Harlech became an important cultural centre due to its annual Music Festivals in the Castle each summer from 1867. Literally thousands flocked to these festivals from all parts of Gwynedd and, on special trains, from Liverpool. Harlech had two main patrons in the 19th century: Sir Robert Williames Vaughan Bart (1768-1843), of Nannau and Samuel Holland MP (1803-1892).

In general, the old landed gentry withdrew from the scene during the early Victorian period. Sir R. W. Vaughan Bart, died in 1843. The mansion and lands of Corsygedol, the district's principal estate, were sold by the Hon E. M. Ll. Mostyn (later the second Lord Mostyn) in the 1840s and 1850s and the subsequent owners (chiefly the Ansell family) played no significant part in Harlech's affairs, though they owned property in the town and several farms in the vicinity. For their part, the owners of Glyn Cywarch, members of the Ormsby and Ormsby-Gore families, were absentees throughout the 19th century. They spent most of their time on their Shropshire lands (Porkington-Brogyntyn), but one of their number was created the first Lord (Baron) Harlech in 1876, an honour which was duly celebrated with carefully orchestrated and well-rewarded enthusiasm in the presence of the new lord and his lady and other members of the far-flung gentry.

This was an age of renewal and mounting optimism in Harlech as it was, generally, throughout Gwynedd, Wales and Britain as a whole. The people remained poor, subordinated and deferential but, under native middle-class leadership, they contributed significantly to the physical and moral improvement of their town. Harlech became a bastion of Nonconformity, a kind of spiritual self-help, and the headquarters of the district's Ivorites, a friendly society or benefit club, formed in 1840, which asserted the principle of self-help in temporal matters. The new mood was also expressed in Liberalism and demands for improved educational and other provision.

Another, and less welcome form of self-help was emigration to the United States, Australia and, later, to Canada. Harlech people also migrated to south Wales and to England in the second half of the century. Those who left were by no means the poorest and the gaps created were not easily filled.

The ancient 'highway' between Dolgellau and Harlech was scarcely more than a cart track in 1800. From Bontddu, it took to the uplands before descending, past the mansion of Corsygedol, to lower ground at Talybont where travellers could refresh themselves at Llanddwywe Inn, on the seaward side of the parish church. The 'road' then proceeded along the present route, apart from the stretch between Llanbedr and Pensarn, to Llanfair, where it again took to higher ground and so down, past Pant Mawr, into Harlech. Some improvements were effected in 1765 at the behest of William Vaughan of Corsygedol and some milestones bearing that date are still to be seen. The Quarter Sessions were responsible for general maintenance until 1833, when the Barmouth and Harlech Turnpike Trust was formed to develop a new road between Barmouth and Talybont, and to improve the existing route from Talybont to Harlech. The Trust was financed by local investors and tolls but the Hon E. M. Ll. Mostyn, the owner of Corsygedol since 1830, made substantial donations. The Ffestiniog and Maentwrog Turnpike Trust was also formed in 1833. The results were quite dramatic: from having some of the worst roads in Wales, Ardudwy soon came to possess some of the best. Just three toll-gates were set up by the former Trust, one at Barmouth and two at Harlech (Clogwyn-Twtil and Llechwedd), and the tolls were farmed out, a common practice, to the highest bidders at annual public auctions. In 1851 the two Trusts were merged and the new Trust was eventually wound up in 1882.

These road improvements were belated yet timely, since they paved the way for the introduction of express coaching services between Caernarfon and Barmouth (Uxbridge Arms-Corsygedol Arms) *via* Harlech. In fact, the *Mountaineer Coach* service was inaugurated in 1833 when the road works must surely have still been in progress. The journey took eight hours on alternate days (Sundays excepted). Harlech became an important staging centre and, anticipating this, Sir R. W. Vaughan Bart, in about 1830, provided the town with a splendid new coaching inn, the Blue Lion, so named because the Nannau family crest was a blue lion rampant. The gentry frowned upon mere trade, but inns and their profits were an exception.

The Blue Lion Inn was built from the shell of Plas yn Harlech, and the early innkeepers, Morgan Davies and Daniel Parry, were carefully selected by Sir Robert. Daniel Parry had this advertisement inserted in the *Herald* in 1833:

'BLUE LION INN, HARLECH, MERIONETHSHIRE. DANIEL PARRY, Begs respectfully to inform the Public, more particularly Tourists and Families visiting this part of the Principality, that he has entered the above Inn which commands a fine view of the old Castle, the ruins of which still continue to attract strangers from various parts of the kingdom, the whole extent of Cardigan Bay [on a clear day!], and the Carnarvonshire Mountains. The town of Harlech lies midway between Tany-bwlch and Barmouth, being about eleven miles distant from each, and it is connected with the former two places by a new road just completed [?]. GOOD STABLING AND LOCK-UP HOUSES, Wines, Spirits, &c. Posting in all its Branches. The Key of the Castle is kept at the Blue Lion.' (*C. & D. H.* 13 July 1833)

This was modernisation indeed, and a far cry from the conditions described by Warner, Evans and others in 1798. The Blue Lion remained Harlech's principal inn (hotel) throughout the 19th century, and it survives today as Plas Cafe. Later landlords and landladies included John Foulkes, who died in 1847; his widow Sarah (1800-1872), who was also the town's postmistress for some years; Hugh Roberts (1805-1868), who seems to have been Sarah Foulkes' brother-in-law; and, following her husband's death by drowning in Cardiff Docks, Mrs Martha Carroll (1851-1907), mother of Edward (Ted) Carroll, marine engineer and landlord of the 'new' Lion Hotel (the former Harp Tavern). The town's reputation as a tourist centre was greatly enhanced.

The turnpike did not pass along what is now Harlech's main street. At the Clogwyn toll-gate the road proceeded through Pentre'r Efail and down Tryfar to Ty'n-y-Groes, where it turned sharply up Twtil (Toot-hill), past the Castle, and out of the town along Llechwedd. How four-horse mail coaches negotiated the sharp bend and steep slope, in either direction, all but beggars the imagination. However, coaches were brought to the front or seaward side of the Blue Lion on a service road (now a grassed terrace) where passengers alighted. Harlech's main street was not a thoroughfare for coaches. On Saturdays it was lined with market stalls and on fair days this unpaved road would have been full of cattle, horses and other livestock, dealers, drovers, farmers, hucksters and all manner of people drawn to the fair to buy, sell (and, sometimes, to steal) or merely to wander around and meet friends.

The town's location still restricted its commercial development to serving the immediate locality. Open-air markets tended to go out of favour during the century and shops became the main retail outlets. Local shops dealt in local produce and in goods imported from Liverpool and elsewhere on locally owned sailing vessels and small steamers such as the *Rebecca*, the *Telephone* and the *Dora*. In the second half of the century the main shops were Cambrian House ('Siop Ffoster'); Gwyndy Stores (later known as 'Siop Denman'); 'Siop y Post' (now Barclays Bank), the Post Office which stocked groceries and drapery, the latter upstairs; Waterloo House where Mrs Catherine Lloyd sold groceries; Clogwyn Shop kept by Rees Evans (a native of Cardigan) who was a building contractor and lay preacher and, at the foot of Twtil, London House, which was named by Captain William Williams, master of the brig *Unity*, who had lived in Southwark in the early 1820s. Gwalia Stores was later opened by Samuel Williams, 'Sam Postman', a noted choirmaster. The inns and taverns were the Blue Lion (Lion Hotel), Clogwyn Inn, the Harp tavern (later renamed the Lion Hotel), the White Horse Inn (next to the Harp), the Castle Hotel (opened in 1876), the Belle Vue Hotel and the Queen's Hotel, a railway hotel near the station. Harlech also had a 'Gin Shop' (now the Castle Cottage Restaurant) but it was a butcher's shop by the 1880s. The town also possessed at least one Temperance Hotel. In the second half of the century a branch of the North and South Wales Bank (now the Midland Bank) was opened.

Harlech's annual fairs were considered important by the townspeople. They were mainly cattle fairs, though horses were also sold. Cattle were offered for sale on a small plot of ground below the path of St Tanwy's church. When Mr Hatton Wood enclosed this plot with a stone wall in about 1891 a protracted dispute arose. The townspeople claimed that the plot was public ground (there was a public open-air washery nearby) and that it had been wrongfully enclosed. By that time, however, the cattle mart had been moved down to the railway sidings near the station.

Each spring and autumn hiring fairs were held. Men and women were hired as farm servants for periods of six months (*'tymor'* = a season or term). These continued until well into the present century, when the number of farm workers in the district dwindled and the family farm became the norm. Since Harlech served the western parts of Ardudwy, literally

hundreds of men and women attended. General economic conditions were of critical importance:
'HARLECH FAIR. — On Monday, the 11th inst., at this annual gathering, there was an immense concourse of men and women, who came for the purpose of hiring, but owing to the depressed state of agriculture the demand was languid and wages lower.' (*C. & D.H.* 16 November 1850)

According to John Gorton's *Topographical Dictionary* of 1833, Harlech possessed eight annual fairs which were held on 4 March, 19 April, the first Thursday after Trinity Sunday, 30 June, 21 August, 22 September, 10 November and 11 December (unless any of the dates fell on a Sunday, when adjustment was made). The cattle fairs were quite basic to the town's economy, yet bad weather, a poor attendance of dealers and drovers, or the holding of other fairs in the general locality (*eg:* at Penmorfa) on or near the same day often meant the farmers had to take their cattle home. The September fair in 1859, for example, proved most disappointing:
'There was an unusual number of beasts, but a paucity of drovers, consequently the demand was sluggish. Best three year old runts may be quoted at £12 10s. to £13 . . . The horse fair was a failure . . . Most of the cattle returned home unsold, a circumstance that necessarily dampened the spirits of the farmers, as they were all short of provender.' (*C. & D. H.* 24 September 1859)
Before the completion of the coast railway in 1867 black cattle (usually 'runts') were gathered into herds, shod by cattle farriers and driven into England. Many beasts were sold at Leicester and Northampton, while others were driven on to marts around London: Romford in Essex; Barnet, which was noted for its Welsh cattle and horse fairs, and Brentford, Blackheath and other places. John Robert (1748-1828) of Harlech was a cattle drover as were at least two of his eight sons, Robert ('Robin') and John. John Roberts junior (born 1793), of Maesgwyn, Harlech, remained a drover or 'driver' in 1851. The elder John Robert had married Mary Griffith (1764-1841) at Llandanwg in April 1790. In April 1816, he wrote to his wife at Harlech, in Welsh of course, from an inn or tavern in England called the Three Rabbits. Times were hard and it was a cold April. This translated extract conveys a sense of the man:
'The cattle are too expensive from thirty shillings to two pounds a head. After all I am glad there are so few. It is a bad time for everybody . . . I fear that pain and tribulation will lead me to the grave. I try to be satisfied with my lot. It is difficult enough for lots of people. If Robin buys any in Harlech he knows what sort to buy better than I do. This briefly from you kind husband ["caredig Briod"] . . . Remember me to my friends and all the children . . .'
He noted that he had received a letter from his son Robin in Leicester and he instructed his wife to 'keep turning the land without expecting anything from me' and to 'plant potatoes in a piece of the upper corner of Cae Penybryn'.

The completion of the coast railway in 1867, with junctions near Barmouth (Barmouth Junction — Morfa Mawddach) and at Afonwen, led to drastic changes in the cattle trade and soon put the remaining drovers out of business. At Harlech, two dealers, John Williams and William Edmunds, switched their operations from the fairs to the mart near the station. Harlech ceased to be a Welsh Abilene and its main street became cleaner and less odorous!

The people of Harlech, schooled in subordination and deference, began to assert themselves, under middle-class leadership, in the 19th century. Nonconformity was an important expression of this new popular mood and the formation of the Ivorites friendly society or benefit club, 'Gwir Iforiaid Caer Collwyn', was another. The Ivorites, named in honour of Ifor Hael, were distinctively and proudly Welsh, and the Harlech lodge was formed in 1840 by a small group of local landowners, Anglican clergymen and a tenant farmer, Lewis Thomas of Llandanwg farm. In return for monthly subscriptions (initially 1s 2d) members received payments to cover periods of sickness (including medical fees), burial expenses and the like. The early members were mainly tenant farmers, master mariners, tradesmen and so on, but quarrymen soon joined and became an influential element. The poor looked on, excluded by their poverty from this beneficial institution. Women (Iforesau) were admitted soon after 1840 and payments (7s) were also made with respect to confinements ('esgoreddiadau') of members' wives. In 1868 the office holders were: Ellis Pugh, farmer and tanner, president ('Llywydd'); John R. Edwards, shopkeeper, secretary ('Ysgrifenydd'); and John R. Pugh, shopkeeper, president of the eisteddfod ('Llywydd y Cyfeisteddfod'), which was held each year in the Castle. In that year, ten payments were made towards burial expenses and, quite typically, eight involved the burial of children.

The annual meetings of the Harlech Ivorites (membership extended to Porthmadog and Barmouth) were quite regularly reported in the local press. For example, in May 1845, after the accounts had been inspected, the Ivorites 'went in procession (the band playing the Men of Harlech) to the New Church' and after the service, the men (180) dined at the Blue Lion Hotel and the women ('about 140') at the White Horse. The procession then reformed and the Ivorites' proceeded in regular order, with drums beating and colours flying, through the streets of the town and around the walls of the old Castle, the band playing as before'. They assembled inside the Castle beneath 'a beautiful flag' (arranged by James Anwyl, then custodian of the Castle) and were addressed by leading members, Rev Rees Evans of Llanfair, R. H. Richards Esq, of Llanfair Isaf (two of the society's founders) and Mr John Griffith, tanner, 'on the indispensable necessity of providing, when young and in health, for the wants of old age, and of affording actual relief in cases of illness and accidents' (*C. & D. H.* 22 May 1845). Many members then accompanied members of the Criccieth Ivorites to Mochras 'where they embarked again for Carnarvonshire'. Whit Monday was the most favoured day for such annual gatherings. The Ivorites' financial and other records were kept scrupulously in Welsh at a time when the language was coming under fire from ill-informed sources.

Another form of self-help, for the middle section of local society, was emigration to the United States (Wisconsin and, later, Kansas) and migration (south Wales and England).

In 1851 the census reveals that the parish contained 119 occupied dwellings, some of which were divided into attics, ground-floor tenements and basements or cellars. The inhabitants numbered 565 (283 males and 282 females) most of whom lived in the town. There were eight households at Bethel (long since demolished) containing 34 people; nine at Porkington Alley ('Rali' — later renamed Porkington Terrace) with 28 people, and nine at Penybryn with 41 people. The old Shire/Town Hall then contained two households and five people. Most lived within the uncertain bounds of the old borough or at Pentre'r Efail.

No less than 41 farming tenements were listed in 1851 and four of the farmers were women. The holdings ranged from five acres (London House) to 195 acres (Erw Wen, an upland farm). James Anwyl (1794-1875) of the former Red Lion Inn, shopkeeper and custodian of the Castle, farmed some 40 acres. The common occupations were farm servant, farm labourer, dairy maid and domestic servant (all women). Five of the seven bakers were women as were all three lodging-house keepers. One woman was a butter merchant. The mariners included William Lewis (1833-1882) of Pencerrig, Harlech, aged 18, who later commanded the schooner *Confidence* of Porthmadog and was rewarded for his services to Garibaldi in the 1860s; Robert Jones Evans (1819-1867) of Fronwen, who was drowned off Monte Video when master of the barque *Samuel* of Liverpool. Some men and boys worked in the slate mines of Ffestiniog. The small slate mine at Llanfair was opened in the late 1850s. Others were craftsmen and tradesmen. They included six shoemakers (another six were then employed at Ty'n Llan, Llanfair), six stone masons, three butchers, three blacksmiths and a pit sawyer, a mole catcher and a corn miller. There were also five tailors and a watchmaker, William James Davies, a son of the schoolmaster. A few women were employed as straw bonnet makers, stocking knitters, dressmakers and milliners, woollen spinners and laundresses. There were 36 paupers listed (30 females, mostly widows). In short, Harlech was a working class community in which those who could not support themselves bore the stigma of pauperism as recipients of 'outdoor relief' or, worse still, as inmates of the Workhouse at Penrhyndeudraeth, opened in about 1840. There was no resident doctor or lawyer in 1851: Harlech was a town with scarcely a hint of urbanity.

Later censuses convey a broadly similar impression and *Slater's Directory* of 1880 contains useful additional information. In 1881 no fewer than 51 slate quarry workers were listed, among them Andrew Nelson, a Swede! Some women broke out of their restrictive roles and none more so than Mrs Mary Lloyd (1846-1917) of Belle Vue, who owned and managed the three-masted schooners *Theda* (to 1893) and *Mary Lloyd* (from 1894) of Porthmadog. She generally employed Harlech men and boys, including her three sons by a former marriage (to Captain Griffith Arthur Jones). The few English residents in 1881 included William Lovegrove, the first landlord of the Castle Hotel and his family; the Deakin brothers of Birmingham, artists, at Bronwen Terrace; and Joseph Shuttleworth, a Yorkshireman, who was a house painter. Sarah Lewis, aged 23, an assistant in Rees Evans' shop at Clogwyn, was a native of Berlin, Wisconsin.

The ancient sand-girt parish church at Llandanwg continued to serve the reduced Anglican congregation of Harlech until the new church, St Tanwg's, was built in the town in 1839-40 on land provided by Sir R. W. Vaughan Bart, of Nannau. The resident congregation remained small until it was increased by members of the new English ascendancy and their servants towards the close of the century, but the incumbents, rectors, were prominent figures in this essentially Nonconformist community. Several chapels were built and enlarged: *Ainon* replaced the Baptist *Bethel* in about 1870 and was replaced by *Tabernacl* (now a Toyota car showroom) in 1896-7; *Moreia* was enlarged and a cemetery was added for the Calvinistic Methodists; the Wesleyans had their *Seion* rebuilt in 1871 with the aid of a loan from the Manchester circuit; and the Independents' *Jerusalem* was built in 1881. In 1811, the Baptist congregation at *Bethel* was split when several families, influenced by J. R. Jones of *Ramoth* (Llanfrothen), broke away to join the Scotch Baptists ('Bedyddwyr Albanaidd'). *Rehoboth*, or 'Capel Uchaf', was built in 1820 for these 'Batîs Bara a Chaws' (Bread and Cheese Baptists) on the hill overlooking the town. Sermons were delivered by lay preachers (commonly elders or deacons — 'Blaenoriaid'). A regular preacher was Edward Humphreys (1830-1886), tailor, of Harlech and another was Morris Rowlands (1817-1897), a blacksmith in Llanfair. They were also assistant relieving officers, under the Poor Law of 1834, for the parishes of Llandanwg and Llanfair respectively. An early member of this congregation was Henry Jones (1781-1861), shipbuilder and sailmaker of Porthmadog, whose wife Margaret was a native of Harlech.

Relations between Anglicans and Nonformists at Harlech were sometimes strained but a fair amount of mutual respect existed. Many Ivorites were Nonconformists, yet they attended annual services at St Tanwg's and sometimes at Llanfair. Captain Lewis Holland Thomas of Caerffynnon Hall, Talsarnau, grandfather of Sir Lewis Casson, a former master mariner who had made a goodly sum in property deals in San Francisco during the Gold Rush era, was particularly enlightened. An Anglican and a Tory, he supported a variety of good causes irrespective of their religious affiliations and, in return, people even forgave him his political allegiance at a time when Welshness, Nonconformity and Liberalism seemed to most to be indivisible. Religion was central to people's lives, and the chapels were not simply places of worship, but popular academies and even centres of entertainment, for powerful preachers attracted large gatherings of the faithful from a wide area.

The Harlech Endowed School, founded in 1665, emerges from obscurity in the 19th century. Evan Anwyl, who left the sea to become a grocer in his native town, was the schoolmaster in the 1820s. In 1831, Evan James Davies (1777-1849), who had been master of the Dyffryn school for many years, was appointed master at Harlech, and he retained the post until shortly before his death. The school was inspected by Assistant-Commissioner John James, a native of Merioneth, for the Royal Commission on Education in Wales which reported in 1847. James came to Harlech on 17 December 1846. Five girls and 20 boys were then enrolled and all the boys were present. The subjects taught were reading, writing and arithmetic and, to the 'free scholars', the Church Catechism. Fees for the pay scholars ranged from 5s to 8s per quarter, and instruction in navigation cost £2. There were two navigation students in 1846. The school was held in the master's dwelling. The room had one window and could not be properly ventilated. John James noted that the master spoke English 'pretty well' and that 'some of the older pupils have a tolerable acquaintance with that language'. Discipline was described as 'very bad'. E. J. Davies was then 69 and 'partially deaf'. He had been a teacher for 'upwards of forty years' and had previously been employed in a warehouse in London. He had never been trained to teach. John James concluded that 'The little knowledge which I discovered among his pupils appeared to have been acquired by rote'. The Charity Commissioners had noted, in 1836, that E. J. Davies received an annual salary of £10 for teaching twelve poor children nominated by the rector and churchwardens of the parish (*ie:* the modest rental of Rhuddallt farm in Llanaber parish). He then paid £2 a year for his cottage schoolroom (possibly Caereinion at Penllech), so he clearly relied on pay scholars to supplement his meagre income. John James maintained in 1846 that the one effective school between Maentwrog and Barmouth was at Llanbedr, some three miles south of Harlech.

In spite of these adverse comments the school's 'alumni' included Captain David Evans (1817-1895) who, after a distinguished career in the merchant service, served with distinction in the US Revenue Marine from 1863 to 1885 before retiring to his home in Berlin, Wisconsin. Another former pupil, John Lloyd (1826-1911) of Cwm Bychan, was a pioneer, in 1870/1, of Bala township in Riley County, Kansas. Evan James Davies's son, William James Davies (1811-1880), was Harlech's clock and watchmaker and, for many years, secretary of the local Ivorites. Perhaps their native intelligence overcame the limitations of their schooling or E. J. Davies may have been a better teacher than John James believed.

Henry Hughes, son of Harlech's chemist and druggist Hugh H. Hughes, was schoolmaster for some years from 1849 and the last master of the Endowed School. Maurice Jones (1820-1875), 'Meurig Idris', was a poet of some local note. In 1874, the new Board School was opened at Rock Terrace on a site provided by Samuel Holland MP. The third master, a former pupil, was Daniel Angel Jones MSc FLS, a noted botanist and a son of Daniel Jones of Gwyndy Stores. Dr John Thomas, a pupil, became a leading industrial chemist. Yet some children were withdrawn from the school in the early years for various reasons — 'distance too much in winter', 'too cold in winter', etc. The early registers are a mine of information. The children of Dr Richard Thomas Jones (1854-1924) of Penygarth (now the Youth Hostel) went on to the new County Intermediate School at Barmouth, which was opened in 1894-5, and other Harlech children followed in the early years of the present century, often due to heroic sacrifices by their parents. Dr R. T. Jones, the local general practitioner and a radical-Liberal, became Harlech's first county councillor in 1889.

The completion of the coast railway between Barmouth and Abererch near Pwllheli in 1867 caused great excitement at Harlech as elsewhere. The Aberystwyth and Welsh Coast Railway Company was formed in 1861 and its line to Aberystwyth was opened in July 1864. Late in

1865, James Anwyl of Harlech recorded in his notebook that the first engine had run on the iron road ('y ffordd haiarn') below the town. The original company had then been absorbed by the Cambrian Railways Company. Passengers first travelled on the new line in August 1867. The local cattle trade was transformed as the drovers became largely redundant; large numbers of people were able to attend the annual Music Festivals in the Castle and the parliamentary elections of 1868, 1870 and 1874 at Harlech; the railway also provided a speedier means of migration from the district for those in search of work; and the trains certainly boosted Harlech's seasonal tourist trade. The express coach services between Caernarfon and Barmouth (the *Mountaineer* had been succeeded by the *Tourist*) did not survive for long. This was Askew Roberts' description of the town in his *Gossiping Guide to Wales* in 1882:

'If we arrive by train at Harlech station, the castle we see frowning above us will be the one great object of our immediate desire. But how to achieve it? The railway company has landed us on the flats, and we want to reach the heights. An omnibus would give the station an air of civilization, but chaises-à-porteurs would carry us to the village — we beg pardon — "county town", more easily. So far we have neither. But now for the castle, en route for the hotels . . . the ruins of the castle are very extensive, and in the courtyard monster concerts are held in the present age . . . The town possesses no trade to speak of, and is compensated by thronging tourists in the season, who make a short halt in the place to enjoy the delightful views and rambles the neighbourhood affords. A new hotel, called (and close to the gates of) the Castle, has recently been erected, and lodging houses are springing up, which looks as if the wives of the Men of Harlech intend to make the visits of Saxon strangers more than short halts. The sea is about a mile from the town, and the bathing place can be approached by a tram car from near the railway station. The shore is remarkable for its sand dunes and the hull of the *Turkestan*, wrecked here a few years ago, is a conspicuous object, to sharp eyes, even from the summit of Snowdon.'

By 1882 much of the small town had been physically transformed at the behest of Samuel Holland MP.

Reform was in the air in the 1830s and the passage of the Reform Bill in 1832, a measure supported by some of Gwynedd's gentry (including the Hon E. M. Ll. Mostyn), unleased a wave of pent-up emotion. Sir R. W. Vaughan Bart, of Nannau, Hengwrt and Rûg, the member for Merioneth, unopposed since 1792, was greatly disturbed by the new mood and decided to resign his seat in 1836. The ceremonial chair upon which he had been carried around Harlech on thirteen occasions as 'knight of the shire' was added to the family heirlooms at Nannau. Sir Robert then arranged the election of his successor as Tory MP, Richard Richards Esq, of Caerynwch, near Dolgellau, the barrister son of Chief Baron Richards of the Court of Exchequer. But first, Richards had to be formally nominated in Harlech's ancient Shire Hall. It soon became apparent that there would be a contest. The Reform candidate was Sir William Wynn, a younger son of the Maesyneuadd family and a soldier.

The scenes in the Shire Hall, Harlech, when the candidates were nominated, were worthy of the pen of Charles Dickens. This was how the *Herald* reported the proceedings:

'Only fancy "the gentry, clergy, and freeholders" of the county of Merioneth huddled up in a close room twelve yards long, six yards wide, and seven feet high; no emblems of official dignity to denote the presence of the Sheriff, except a cracked trumpet . . .; a pot-house chair, and a deal table, sans pens, ink, sans paper and sans every thing but the dignity of uselessness, being the only furniture; gentry, clergy, freeholders, and other electors, sheriff, candidates, nominators, lawyers, reporters, &c. all elbowing, squeezing, and wriggling in the most glorious confusion, and we have only a faint portraiture of the opening of the County Court of Merionethshire at the first contested election for half a century . . . We say little of the confusion of tongues . . . the room in which they were assembled was so like the Black Hole of Calcutta . . .' (*C. & D. H.* 25 June 1836)

Polling took place, in 'commodious booths', on 24 and 25 June, at five centres: Harlech, Dolgellau, Bala, Tywyn and Corwen. Richard Richards won by 501 votes to 150. Following the proclamation a few days later, the new MP was chaired from the Shire Hall to the Blue Lion 'in a plain oak chair, without any decorations, and in comparitive silence'. This muted reception was ominous for the Tory cause in the county. An attempt was made in 1836 to remove these ceremonies from Harlech to Dolgellau, but Sir Robert Williames Vaughan and his friends would not hear of it. Merioneth politics then began to lose their managed predictability as Liberalism gained ground. Even the usually genial Sir Robert was referred to, not without reason, as the 'Merioneth Autocrat' by his political opponents, but he deserves to be remembered as Harlech's one true benefactor in bleak times.

David Williams (1799-1869) of Castell Deudraeth, a wealthy attorney, contested the elections of 1859 and 1865 for the Liberal Party, but his Tory opponents, by dint of intimidation and other devices known collectively as the 'screw', retained their grip on the county. Then, in 1868, with the support of newly enfranchised electors in the quarrying districts of Ffestiniog and south Merioneth, the Liberals gained an astounding victory. The Tory candidates and previous MP, W. R. M. Wynne of Peniarth, capitulated and withdrew from the contest and the elderly David Williams, 'King David', was proclaimed MP for Merioneth at Harlech amid scenes of unprecedented rejoicing. Thousands attended the proclamation ceremony by means of the new coast railway. He then addressed the crowd, first in English and then in Welsh, and many speeches followed. 'Meurig Idris', the town's schoolmaster, recited some *englynion* (verses in strict metre) in honour of the occasion, and David Williams was chaired in triumph through the town. The final words of his speech had been: 'It has been the people's battle in every respect', and so it may have seemed, though the real victors were the new middle-class leaders of Merioneth, and of Wales in general. For Harlech it was a unique occasion, and the town was garlanded with evergreens, flags and other favours in celebration.

Samuel Holland (1803-1892), a wealthy quarryowner and Harlech's main benefactor in this period, succeeded David Williams as MP in 1870. His Tory opponent was Colonel Tottenham. Holland polled 1,610 votes to Tottenham's 936. The Tories again employed the 'screw', but the proclamation ceremony at Harlech passed off without serious incident so that the services of 16 police officers under Inspector Williams of Pwllheli 'were so little required that he sent many of them home at an early hour'. When trains approached the station that morning 'the air reverberated with rock cannon, and the detonators placed on the rails went off crack after crack'. Holland's carriage was met on the Talsarnau road, 'a long distance from Harlech', the horses were removed, and the new member and his lady were drawn to the town by strong men. Harlech was again *en fête*.

Holland retained the seat until 1884-5, but the election of 1874 was to be Harlech's last. It was a dull affair compared with those of 1868 and 1870. This was due in part to the fact that Holland was unopposed, though the 'Secret Ballot' (introduced in 1872) was thought to have been a contributory factor. Some banners were put up, and on Gwyndy Stores Daniel Jones had placed the motto 'Holland, Harlech and Progress'. The member was chaired through the town on an 'old-fashioned chair, covered with blue velvet and decorated with white favours' and 'Meurig Idris' recited an appropriate *englyn*. It was reported, however, that the oldest inhabitants 'shook their heads in utter incredulity that the great election days should be so changed that all which was left was a dumb show'. The next election was celebrated at Dolgellau, and Harlech thus lost its last vestige of county status.

Samuel Holland, a Liverpool-born but Welsh-speaking quarryowner, was Harlech's great benefactor in the 1860s and 1870s. He acquired much of the town and proved to be an enlightened landlord. Cottages and workshops (including the smithy) were improved; lodging-houses were built along the main street (including Gorffwysfa as a Temperance Hotel); Noddfa (Haven) was built as a convalescent home for quarrymen; and the Castle Hotel was opened in 1876 — all at Holland's behest. He was responsible for the new Bronwen Terrace and the more modest Rock Terrace and, in 1878, he provided the horse-drawn tramway which ran, initially, from below Bronwen Terrace to the beach. He also provided the land for the Board School in 1874. As a dedicated temperance reformer, Samuel Holland was one of the main sponsors of the Ardudwy United Temperance Choral Society, which held its first annual concert in the Castle in 1867. These concerts, attended by thousands right from the start, were to blossom into the famous Harlech Music Festivals of the 1920s. Other early sponsors were Lewis Holland Thomas of Caerffynnon Hall, Talsarnau, and his son-in-law Thomas Casson of Porthmadog, banker. Harlech's town band (initially brass) was then under the direction of a certain 'Lawrens Bach' (Little Lawrence) reputedly an uncle of the Tremadog-born T. E. Lawrence, 'Lawrence of Arabia'.

The town which Samuel Holland reconstructed (sadly, his architectural taste was poor) was the town that the poet Robert von Ranke Graves knew as a boy, and described in his *Goodbye To All That* (1929).

POST OFFICE, at the Blue Lion Inn, John Foulkes, *Post Master*.—Letters from all parts (CORWEN, BALA, DOLGELLEY and BARMOUTH excepted) arrive every morning at half-past one, and are despatched every night at half-past eight.—Letters from the places above excepted arrive every night at half-past eight, and are despatched every morning at half-past one.

GENTRY AND CLERGY.

Evans Rev. David (rector), Tymawr
Foster Miss Elizabeth, Penbryn
Humphreys Capt. Humphrey, Llanfair hill [ruchaf
Humphreys Mrs. Jane, Llanfair
Jones John, Esq. Gafelnewydd
Owen Miss Laurie, Fronfair
Richards Richard Humphrey, Esq. Llanfairesa

INNS & PUBLIC HOUSES.

Blue Lion Inn (and posting house), John Foulkes
Clogwyn, John Roberts
White Horse, John Jones

SHOPKEEPERS & TRADERS.

Anwyl Evan, grocer & linen draper
Davies Evan Jas. master of charity school [maker
Davies William Jas. clock and watch
Evans Rees, baker
Griffiths Roberts, tailor
HARLECH SLATE COMPANY, Harlech Slate Quarries—William Williams, agent
Jones Abraham, stone mason
Jones David, joiner
Jones John, joiner
Jones Owen, tinman and glazier
Jones Owen, stone mason
Jones Owen, miller
Jones Richard, cooper
Lloyd Edmund, grocer & tea dealer
Lloyd Robert, turner
Owens Jane, grocer and tea dealer
Owens William, clock maker
Owens William, butcher
Parry Henry, tailor
Parry Mary, flour dealer
Pritchard Robert, blacksmith
Richards Evan, glover and skinner
Roberts Michael, shoe maker
Spencer Robert, shoe maker
Thomas Owen, tailor
Williams Griffith, carpenter
Williams Hugh grocer and draper
Williams Robert, carpenter
Williams Robert, butcher
Williams Robert, shoe maker
Williams William, grocer and draper

COACH.

To ABERYSTWYTH, the *Snowdon* (from Carnarvon) calls at the Blue Lion Inn, every Tuesday, Thursday and Saturday at twelve, during the summer months; goes through Barmouth, Dolgelley and Machynlleth.

To CARNARVON, the *Snowdon* (from Aberystwyth) calls as above, every Monday, Wednesday and Friday afternoon at three, during summer; goes through Tre-Madoc and Beddgelert.

CARRIER.

To CARNARVON, William Roberts, every Friday afternoon; goes through Tre-Madoc and Llanllyfni.

ABOVE: Part of the entry for Harlech in *Pigot and Slater's Directory* for 1844. (GAS) OPPOSITE LEFT: St Tanwg's church, Harlech, built in 1839-40 on land provided by Sir R. W. Vaughan. (MW) RIGHT: An advertisement for the *Mountaineer Coach* between Caernarfon and Barmouth in 1833 from the *Carnarfon Herald*. (UCNWA) BELOW: A view of Harlech by R. P. Leitch and Whymper Sc. The four-horse coach is too far down Toothill (*Twtil*). The cottage (Ty'n-y-Groes) was the turning point.

Mountaineer Coach

FROM CARNARVON TO BARMOUTH;

ALSO, THE

Prince Coach,

AS USUAL, TO MENAI BRIDGE, TO MEET THE STEAM BOATS, MORNING AND EVENING.

THE Public are respectfully informed, that the MOUNTAINEER COACH will leave the UXBRIDGE **ARMS**, CARNARVON, every MONDAY and THURSDAY, at **Eight** in the Morning, and will arrive at BARMOUTH at **Five P. M.**, where all sorts of Conveyances may be had for **Aberystwyth**, &c. &c. On the same days the Coach leaves Barmouth **at Seven A. M.**, and arrives at Carnarvon about Five P. M. **in time** for the Mail Coach for Bangor, or the Morning Coach at **Seven** for the Steam Boats at Menai Bridge.

This Coach goes through some of the most beautiful Scenery in Wales, the new line from Tanybwlch to Harlech and Barmouth **being** completed. The new Carriage Road by the side of the Embankment, and the whole way from Tremadoc to Tanybwlch **is going** on rapidly.

As soon as the roads between Dolgelley and Aberystwyth are **improved**, this public accommodation will be extended to the latter place.

N.B. In last week's paper, the days of starting were, by mis-**take**, stated Monday, Wednesday, and Friday, instead of Monday **and Thursday.**

Uxbridge Arms, Carnarvon, July 26th, 1833.

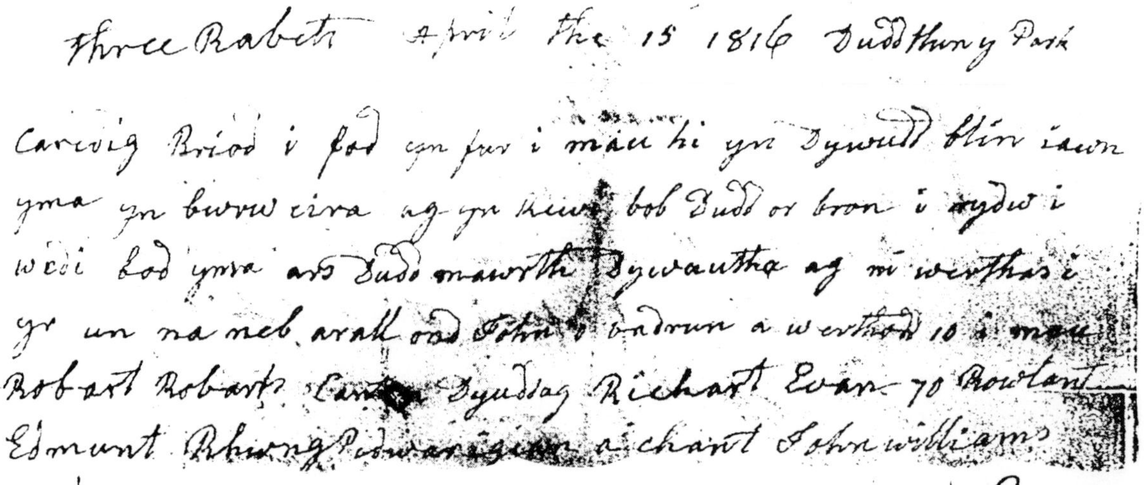

three Robets April the 15 1816 Dudd[illegible] Park

Carwig Briod i fod yn fur i mae hi yn Dywidd [illegible] iawn
yma yn bwrw eira ag yn rhewi bob Dudd or bron i [illegible] i
wedi bod yma ars Dudd mawrth Dywaatha ag mi werthas i
yr un na neb arall oed John [illegible] a werthod 10 i [illegible]
Robert Roberts [illegible] Dyudday Richart Evan 70 Rowlant
Edmunt [illegible] a chant John williams

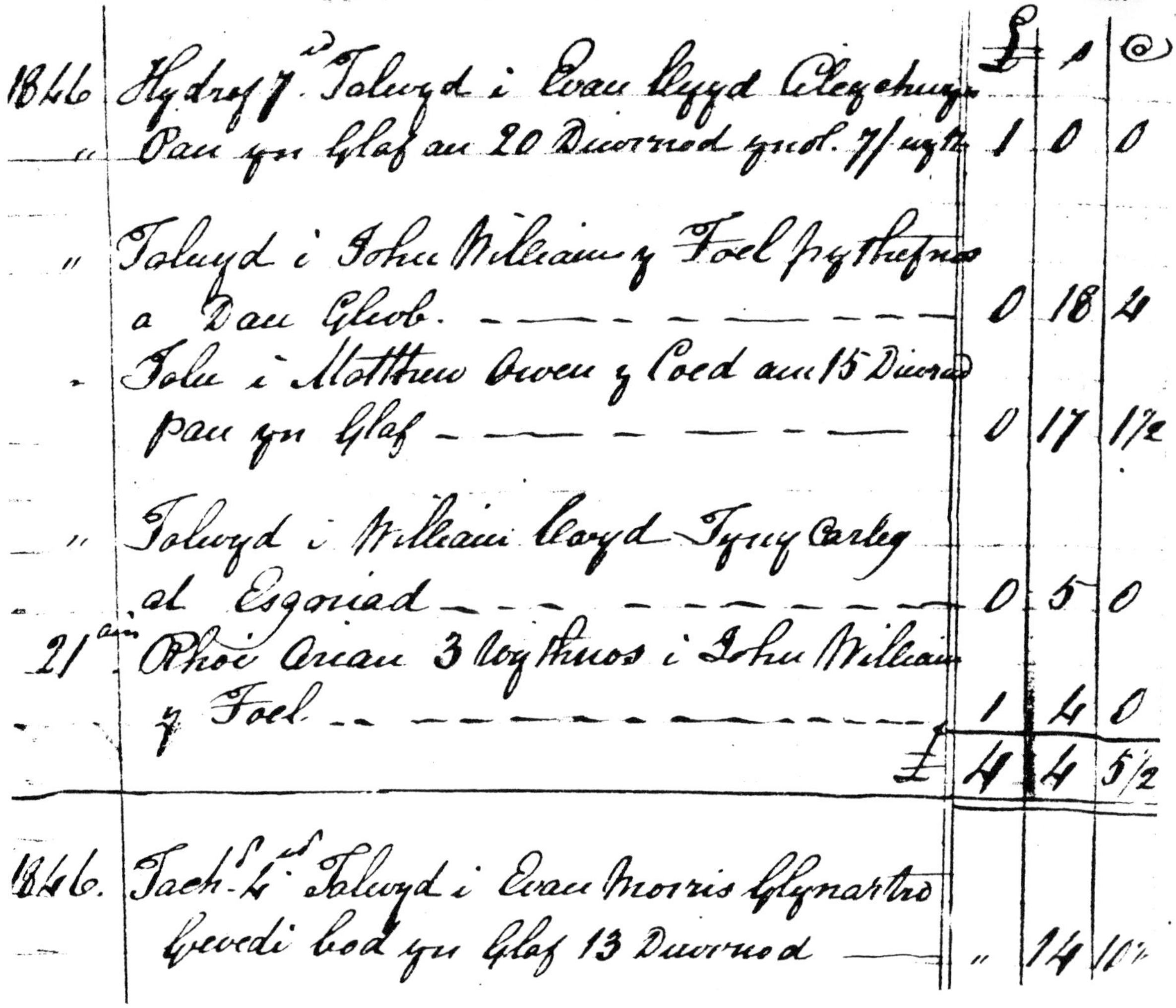

		£	s	d
1846	Hydref 7ed Talwyd i Evan Lloyd [illegible] Pan yn Glaf am 20 Diwrnod ynol 7/ wyth.	1	0	0
"	Talwyd i John William y Foel pythefnos a Dau Glwb.	0	18	4
"	Talu i Matthew Owen y Coed am 15 Diwrnod pan yn Glaf	0	17	1½
"	Talwyd i William Lloyd Tynycarleg at Esgoriad	0	5	0
21ain	Rhoi Arian 3 Wythnos i John William y Foel	1	4	0
	£	4	4	5½
1846.	Tach. 4ed Talwyd i Evan Morris Glynarthro wedi bod yn Glaf 13 Diwrnod	"	14	10½

ABOVE: The cattle drover John Robert(s)'s letter to his wife dated 15 April 1816. (JN and GAS) BELOW: Payments of sickness and other benefits to certain Ivorites in 1846. (GAS)

Ymwelwyr y Cleifion.

Llanfihangel—C. Williams, Talsarnau.
Llandecwyn—Wm. Jones, Penbryn isaf.
Harlech Ogl.—M. R. Richards, Harlech.
„ Dehau—O. Morris, etto
Llanfair—Ellis Lloyd, Llanfair.
Llanbedr isaf—T. Roberts, Pensarn.
Llanbedr ucha—J. Evans, Gof, Penybont
Maentwrog—Humphrey Thomas.
Ffestiniog—W. Evans, Cwmstrallyn.
Portmadoc—Robt. Evans, Tailor.
Dyffryn—Robt. Owen, Dyffryn.

Pwyllgor.

Llywydd—H. Humphreys, Ymwlch
John Williams, Grogan.
Morris Rowlands, Llanfair.
Griffith Owen, Talsarnau.
Owen Morris, Rock Terrace.
Evan Williams, Prysg.
M. R. Richards, Harlech.
Cadwaladr Williams, Talsarnau.
John Williams, Maesgwyn.

Ymddiriedolwyr.

Capt. Edwards, Cae'rgethin.
Mr. Morris Rowlands, Llanfair.
Mr. J. R. Pugh, Llechwedd, Harlech
Mr. Wm. Edmunds, Plas uchaf.
Mr. Humphrey Thomas, Maentwrog

ELLIS PUGH, Llywydd.
JOHN R. EDWARDS, Ysgrifenydd.
JOHN R. PUGH, Llywydd y Cyfeisteddfod.

ABOVE: Officers of the Harlech Ivorites from the printed accounts of 1868. LEFT: Capt William Lewis of Pencerrig, Harlech, master of the schooner *Confidence* of Porthmadog. CENTRE: The silver tankard presented to Capt Lewis by supporters of Garibaldi in London. (All GAS) RIGHT: Capt Humphrey Humphreys (1802-1863), owner and first master of the brig *Lady Vaughan* of Barmouth. (GAP and GAS)

OPPOSITE ABOVE: The brig *Lady Vaughan* of Barmouth launched in 1826 and lost in 1863. Capt Humphreys, the owner, lived at Llanfair Hill. (GAP and GAS) BELOW: The three-masted schooner *Mary Lloyd* of Porthmadog, launched in 1894. The managing owner for many years was Mrs Mary Lloyd of Belle Vue. (GAS) LEFT: Robert Owen (1832-1869) of Harlech, mariner, photographed at Riga. He was lost on voyage from Palermo to Newcastle. (EW) RIGHT: Loading slates at Porthmadog harbour c1890. (GAS) BELOW: Pentre'r Efail, Harlech with Baptist *Capel Ainon* (1870-1896) on the extreme right. (GAS)

LEFT: The Calvinistic Methodist *Capel Moreia* at Tryfer, successor of the original chapel built in 1769. RIGHT: The Wesleyan *Capel Seion* (1871) on Harlech's main street. BELOW: *Capel Rehoboth*, the Scotch Baptists' chapel opened in 1820. (All MW)

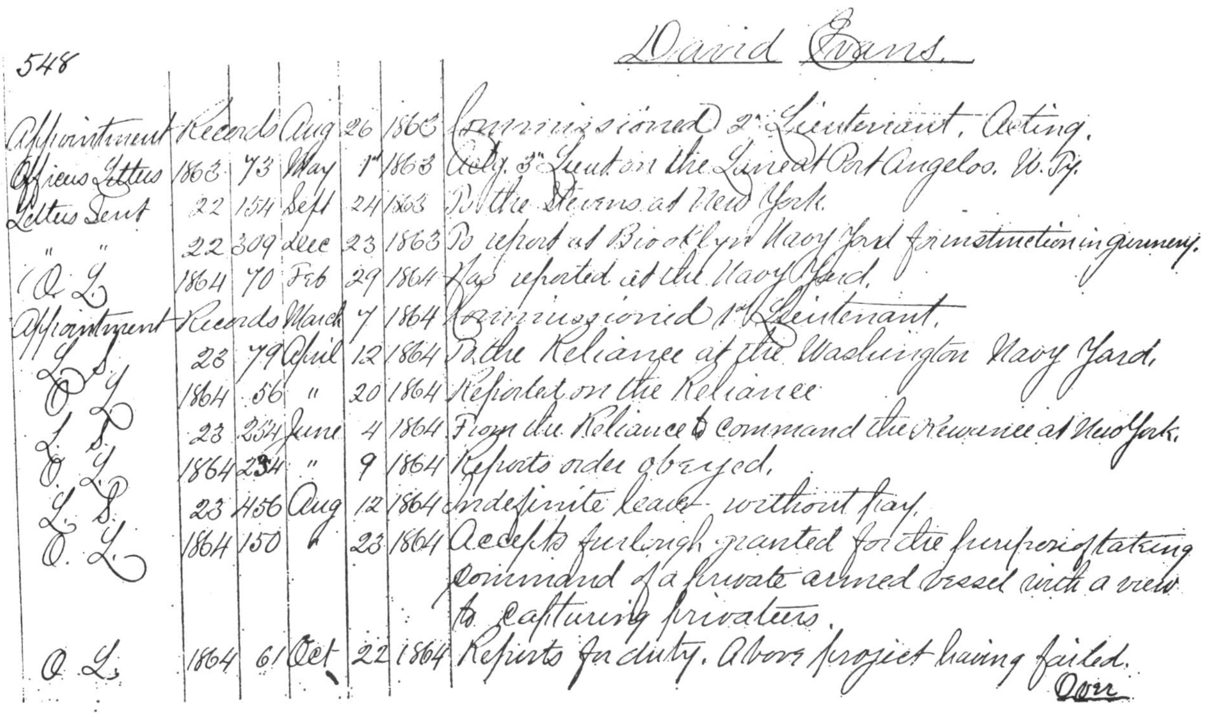

548 David Evans.

Appointment	Records		Aug	26	1863	Commissioned 2nd Lieutenant, Acting.
Officers Letters	1863	73	May	1st	1863	Actg. 3rd Lieut on the Lincoln at Port Angelos. W. T.
Letters Sent	22	154	Sept	24	1863	To the Stevens at New York.
" "	22	309	Dec	23	1863	To report at Brooklyn Navy Yard for instruction in gunnery.
O. L.	1864	70	Feb	29	1864	Has reported at the Navy Yard.
Appointment	Records		March	7	1864	Commissioned 1st Lieutenant.
L. S.	23	79	April	12	1864	To the Reliance at the Washington Navy Yard.
O. L.	1864	56	"	20	1864	Reported on the Reliance
L. S.	23	254	June	4	1864	From the Reliance to command the Reliance at New York.
O. L.	1864	234	"	9	1864	Reports order obeyed.
L. S.	23	456	Aug	12	1864	Indefinite leave without pay.
O. L.	1864	150	"	23	1864	Accepts furlough granted for the purpose of taking command of a private armed vessel with a view to capturing privateers.
O. L.	1864	61	Oct	22	1864	Reports for duty. Above project having failed.

Over

ABOVE: Part of David Evans' Service Record in the U.S. Revenue Marine. (USNA) LEFT: The grave of John Lloyd and his third wife Grace at Bala, Kansas. Grace bore him 12 children to add to the 10 children of his first wife in Wales. (AW) RIGHT: Daniel Angel Jones MSc, FLS, headmaster of the Harlech Board School and his staff c1920.

LEFT: Samuel Holland (1803-1892) MP, Ffestiniog quarryowner, temperance reformer, Merioneth's second Liberal MP and, for several years, Harlech's main benefactor. (GAS) BELOW: Harlech's High Street with Gorffwysfa and beyond it the Lion Hotel, c1890. Samuel Holland's influence is evident. (NLW) RIGHT: London House, the Lower Harlech Post Office, in 1986, so named by Capt William Williams (1783-1868) some time prior to 1851. (MW)

ABOVE: The view from the 'town square' to Penybryn, c1890. Note the Harp Inn and the White Horse immediately above the Harp on the right. (NLW) CENTRE: Holland's Bronwen Terrace in 1986, an enduring row of respectable Victorian houses and superior guesthouses. (MW) BELOW: The castle from the front of Holland's Castle Hotel with visitors in a carriage, c1890. (GAS)

ABOVE: The Castle with the corn mill (right foreground end on), c1890. The mill appears to have been renovated quite recently. BELOW: The gravestone of Sion Phylip of Mochras, poet, at Llandanwg with verses inscribed much later: one of the roots of our strong literary tradition. (GAS)

Harlech's New Ascendancy

During the closing decades of the 19th century several well-to-do English families settled or began to spend the summer months in Ardudwy. Large houses were built to accommodate these newcomers and their domestic servants such as Ael-y-Bryn, Dyffryn, and Hafod-y-Bryn, Llanbedr. Land and labour were cheap and the natives were not merely friendly but generally anxious to please. The town thus became a kind of summer hill station — a Welsh Simla by the Celtic Sea. Members of this new ascendancy, which was superimposed upon the local and native middle class, dispensed patronage in various forms. They supported the annual Music Festivals and the many local choirs which formed their basis; they subscribed to the Harlech Library and Institute, and some sponsored the creation of the Harlech Golf Links, and the associated St David's Hotel. The newcomers included A. P. Graves (1846-1931), an Anglo-Irishman, and his German-Danish wife Amy (1857-1951); W. H. (Harry) More (d1934), who came with his family to Harlech in 1892 as Receiver of Crown Lands for Wales and Monmouthshire, an office which he held until his retirement in 1925; the then Earl of Winchilsea and Nottingham; Lord (Earl) and Lady Amherst, and George Davison, the son of a Norfolk ship carpenter, European director of Eastman-Kodak and a convinced philosophical anarchist (much to the annoyance of George Eastman).

Several imposing new houses were built to accommodate these families: Erinfa (Graves), Crown Lodge (More, though the family lived at Noddfa for several years), Plas Amherst and Plas Wernfawr (Davison). Lord Winchilsea succeeded his uncle, Mr Hatton Wood, to the Nannau lands in Harlech (including Bronygraig and the Blue Lion Hotel where he resided at times). This was a curiously assorted new ascendancy, but they soon became the new patrons of the town in succession to such people as Sir R. W. Vaughan of Nannau, William Ormsby Gore of Glyn Cywarch and Samuel Holland. This was possibly the final expansive phase of the leisured class in Britain and Harlech provided a faithful expression of it, in miniature, for a while. As W. H. More's daughter Constance (Mrs Lyne) recalled in her unpublished memoirs:

'The "County" lived in large houses with great distances between . . . I remember long drives to children's parties, and tennis parties at our own house, at which ladies in long pique skirts, and gentlemen in white flannels dashed about and we children "fielded" balls, and envied them the large teas . . . Of music there was never any dearth, my mother was a good pianist . . . and how good some of the local talent was! . . . Later we had a string quartette . . . Later still there was Lady Winchilsea's picked mixed choir, consisting of all the best voices in the village, and those evenings are golden memories to the few of us who can remember.'

She recalled the main street 'with its grey houses and white-washed cottages' where 'old Janet', Mrs Jennett Williams (1829-1913), widow of Robert Williams, a coachman, used to sit in 'Welsh costume'. Her father took her into the 'small corner shop', Cambrian House, 'its counters filled with vegetables, loaves of bread, plates of oat cake, balls of string, and an enormous pair of scales' and 'The shelves behind held bottles of sweets, tea pots, basins, whip tops and tin canisters. I can see the kindly red faced owner of that shop, and hear his call into the parlour of "Come you here, for to see the little English girl".' Lewis Foster Edwards (1844-1932) and his 'gentle wife' were remembered with special affection by Mrs Lyne: 'F. E. in his black apron and basket on his arm in which he carried his orders to the various houses was a familiar and beloved sight'. She also recalled 'formal dinner parties' at Plas Amherst with their 'long graces before dinner and grace again before the cloth was removed for dessert'. Lady Amherst, who was many years younger than her husband, used to ride with her guests, on Welsh ponies, through the town, 'a gay and glittering cavalcade'. The guests at 'that hospitable house' included E. F. Benson, Lady Cromartie and Lord Sanderson, 'then an old man'.

Some servants were brought to Harlech in this period (and several descendants still live in the area) though many local people were employed. The expression 'being in service' came to possess a special connotation in a district where ordinary domestic servants were still numerous. The newcomers were not ungenerous in their dealings with the Welsh inhabitants though their presence may have encouraged a certain servility, and a touch of envy in a community which was poor but industrious and used to its penury and conventional ways. George Davison of Plas Wernfawr was unconventional in all things and not least in his generosity towards the children and old people of Harlech and its vicinity. Plas Wernfawr was completed in 1908 and the 'Great Hall' was added in 1910. Both were designed by the Scottish architect George Walton. The total cost is reputed to have been £80,000. A large family of orphans was installed and local people were encouraged to use the Great Hall for concerts and other entertainments. George Davison also played host to professional entertainers and George Bernard Shaw visited the mansion when he came, with other leading Fabians, to 'summer schools' at Llanbedr. The newcomers supported the annual Music Festivals and other local events and some of them initiated the Golf Links on Morfa Harlech in 1895:

'The Golf course, later to become famous [as the Royal St. David's under the patronage of the future Duke of Windsor], was laid out by Mr Stormont Finch-Hatton afterwards the Earl of Winchilsea, his brother, Harold Finch-Hatton, and my father. They were advised by John Ball, who played the opening game . . . William Leaver was the first professional, and Mrs Hughes was the first stewardess of the club . . .'

This was how Mrs Lyne recalled a most significant development at Harlech. Lord Winchilsea was the first president and W. H. More was the first honorary secretary of the Club. In 1910 the St David's Hotel was built for some £8,000 to George Walton's interesting design. Lord Winchilsea and George Davison were shareholders. With the completion of the Golf Links, caddying became a source of income for men and children of the town and neighbouring villages. Boys often did three rounds a day to take home 2s 3d (*ie:* 9d a round) as my father, Lewis Pugh Lloyd (1900-1979) recalled. Many famous golfers drew attention to the fine course in its truly superb setting. According to Mrs Lyne they included Bernard Darwin, Mure Ferguson and Harold Hilton.

LEFT: Lewis Pugh (Roberts), boatswain of the brig *Atalanta* of Caernarfon 1864-5, and his wife Mary, c1880. (MPH) RIGHT: The brigantine *Edward Windus* of Porthmadog, a vessel well known to Harlech seamen in the late 19th century. Frank Ellis was second Mate in 1897, before he turned to steamers. (GAS) BELOW: From a painting of the three-masted schooner *Jenny Jones* of Porthmadog. She was owned and commanded by Capt Tom Ellis of Harlech for some years after 1904. (GAS)

Merionethshire, North Wales.

ON THE

West Coast in the Districts of HARLECH, LLANABER, DYFFRYN, BARMOUTH, LLWYNGWRIL, DOLGELLEY, & TRAWSFYNYDD.

Particulars, with Views, Plans, and Conditions of Sale

OF THE

CORS-Y-GEDOL ESTATE

COMPRISING IN ALL ABOUT

11,500 ACRES OF FREEHOLD LAND,

WITH THE

Fine and Interesting Old Mansion of Cors-y-Gedol,

WITH PLEASURE GROUNDS, PARK AND WOODLANDS,

Numerous Farms, Extensive Sheepwalks, Beautiful Lakes and several Rivers noted for their Salmon and Trout Fishing, numerous Small Holdings with considerable prospective value for Building, several Choice Building Sites, Villa Residences and Cottages, Two Factories or Fulling Mills, over 1,300 Acres of Land abutting on the shore of Cardigan Bay which include a Rabbit Warren and the Dyffryn Golf Links, and " Shell Island,"

ABOVE LEFT: From the Sale Book of the Corsygedol Estate (1908); three land sales in this period allowed Harlech people to begin to buy their homes, workshops and farms. RIGHT: Alfred Perceval Graves (1846-1931) of Erinfa. CENTRE: George Davison of Plas Wernfawr, philosophical anarchist, businessman and philanthropist. (CH) BELOW: The 'High Street' looking northwards, c1900. Cambrian House is on the right. (JH/GAS)

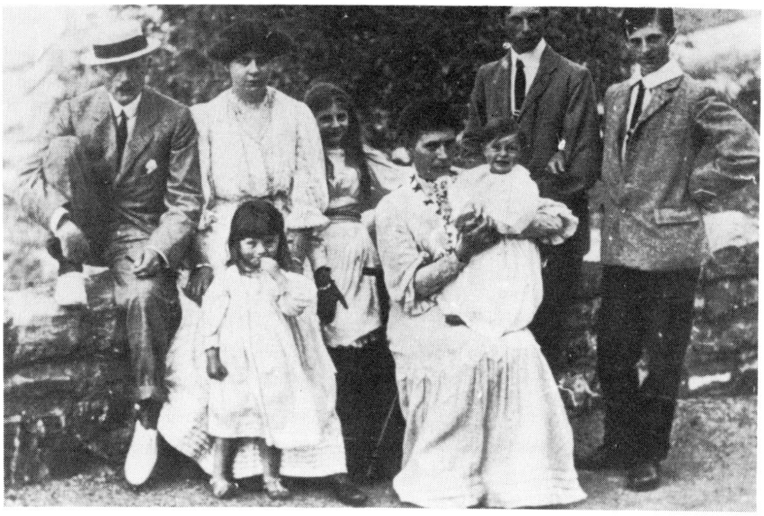

ABOVE: Llanfair primary school children in 1909. Three of the boys were to die in World War I, including William Lloyd (third row back on right). (MPH) LEFT: Five members of the family of Ellis and Ann Loyd, Llanfair: (left to right) Catherine, Mary Pugh, Lewis Pugh, Matthew and William, c1909. RIGHT: W. H. (Harry) More and family at Crown Lodge, c1907. Constance, Mrs Lyne, is seated next to her father. (AB)

ABOVE: Harlech from Pantmawr farm, c1910. (GAS) LEFT: 'Brain Harlech' (Harlech Crows) near Gorffwysfa on the High Street, c1910. (BEE) RIGHT: Ellis Lloyd (1874-1953), c1910. He worked as a miner and quarryman in Ardudwy and in the coal mines of south Wales. (MPH)

ABOVE: The Square, looking south, with motor car registration FF (Merioneth) 132. BELOW: Harlech's postal team outside 'Siop y Post', c1915, with William Ellis (left), who lost an arm in the Transvaal. (JH/GAS)

ABOVE: Samuel Williams ('Sam Postman'), Gwalia Stores, with his youth choir at Penygraig c1920. LEFT: Mrs Ann Rowlands(1853-1938) of Llanfair, shopkeeer, c1930. Her husband, Morris Rowlands junior, blacksmith, had died in 1881. (MPH) RIGHT: The Great Hall of Plas Wernfawr/Coleg Harlech gutted by fire, May 1968. (CH)

LEFT: The St David's Hotel, built in 1910 to George Walton's design, c1920, gutted by fire in 1922. RIGHT: The Humphreys family of Harlech at home in Tonypandy, Rhondda, c1920. Several local families moved to south Wales prior to World War I. (MPH) BELOW: Local men rebuilding the St David's Hotel in the 1920s. (EW)

LEFT: Evan ('Ianto') Humphreys (second from left standing) and other local servicemen photographed at Alexandria, c1918. (MPH) RIGHT: Pte William Lloyd, RWF (standing) and 'Robin Ffatri', Llanbedr. He died of wounds in 1918 aged 19 and was buried at Doullens. (MPH) CENTRE: The King Line's ss *Don Diego*, Capt Frank Ellis's first command, sunk by submarine gunfire 21 May 1917. (GAS) BELOW: The ss *Novgorod*. It was as master of this vessel that Frank Ellis conveyed the first returning soldiers and nurses to be landed at Geelong, Victoria, in 1919. (GAS) INSET: Capt Francis (Frank) Ellis (1876-1971) of Tŷ Mawr, Harlech. (BEE)

Modern Times

The First World War destroyed the serene vision of pre-war days and the last vestiges disappeared during the 'Great Depression' as unemployment accelerated depopulation. That new confidence which had grown in Harlech (as elsewhere) was never regained, despite various attempts at recovery. Besides, the local economy, based on pastoralism, traditional rural crafts, slate quarrying and mining and seafaring, had begun to decline as early as the late 1870s. By 1918, the local economy, with the possible exception of tourism, was in shreds, yet all was not doom and gloom at Harlech in the inter-war years.

The War Memorial at Harlech records the names of 21 young men who died in the 'war to end wars'. They included 2nd Lieutenant Isaac Gwilym Bevers, son of a local schoolmistress, who died of wounds at Yprès in August 1917 aged 24 (a science graduate of UCNW, Bangor); William Owen of Llechwedd Ganol, who was killed at Yprès in January 1915 aged 26, and Private William J. Hughes of Tanyrallt, who served in the 12th Canadian Field Ambulance and died of wounds in France in April 1918. Other memorials, in every village in Ardudwy, record the heavy losses sustained, losses notified by telegrammes which were barely understood by parents with little if any command of English. As volunteers or conscripts, most local men served in the Royal Welch Fusiliers, many on the Western Front and others at Gallipoli and in Mesopotamia. The RWF mustered ultimately 42 battalions, and lost 420 officers and 10,000 men. Several Harlech men served in the Merchant Navy. Captain Frank (Francis) Ellis (1876-1971) was master of the SS *Don Diego* when that vessel was sunk by submarine gunfire on 21 May 1917. William Williams, 'Wil Tallow', of Bronclogwyn, Harlech, was a member of the crew at the time. Frank Ellis's brother William was a chief (marine) engineer during the war. Captain Lewis Lloyd (1876-1917) of Clogwyn Melyn, near Ynys, was lost with the SS *City of Lincoln* in the North Sea on 18 September 1917. The men who returned home commonly bore the physical and mental scars of their ordeal for the rest of their lives. My uncle Evan ('Ianto') Humphreys, who had helped to save the life of John Williams ('Jaci Shop Chips') of Harlech at Gallipoli, came home from the Middle East with a lung wound and later contracted tuberculosis, which killed him in 1927 when he was 32. He and other ex-servicemen formed a branch of the Labour Party in Harlech soon after the war. The Liberal consensus was beginning to break down.

The 'Great Depression' was, in Gwynedd, an intensification of existing general economic decline. Harlech's unemployed sought the solace of snooker in the Institute, which had been opened in 1908, and a few found seasonal work on the golf course. Some migrated to London or other parts of England in search of work as did my father in about 1924. Yet the town still attracted summer visitors and tourists, and the Music Festivals reached new heights with massed choirs of around 1,600 voices under the batons of such renowned conductors as Walford Davies and Edward Elgar (he came just once in 1924). Special trains brought

thousands to Harlech, and the station platforms were greatly extended to accommodate them. And Mrs Constance Lyne noted:
'I remember during one summer Sir Granville Bantock, Joseph Holbrooke, Eugene Goosons [sic], Cyril Scott and Astra Desmond were all in the village together, and on one occasion at a local charity concert the two first named played an arangement for four hands of "Three Blind Mice". I think the setting was by Joseph Holbrooke. I do not know who enjoyed that performance most, the audience or the performers.'
Many other notables came to Harlech after the war, though memories were sometimes confused with recollections of happier pre-war days. The celebrities included the actress Ellen Terry; the writer A. G. Bradley, son of Dean Bradley, and the artists Alexander Poole and Phil Morris RA.

A. P. Graves of Erinfa (lit. Ireland-place) was the principal sponsor of a grand Historical Pageant held in the Castle from 23 to 28 August 1922. Episodes were written by A. P. Graves, Patrick Kirwan, the 'Pageant Master', and Professor J. E. Lloyd. The music was composed by Mr Charles Clements, and Dr Walford Davies was the Musical Director. Many local people took part and they were joined by Lord and Lady Howard de Walden and Megan and Richard Lloyd George, whose father, David Lloyd George, attended the opening performance. However, these post-war effusions were short-lived. The Pageant was not repeated, and the Music Festivals ended in 1932. A. P. Graves died in 1931. An MA and LittD of Trinity College, Dublin, his gravestone in St Tanwg's churchyard records him as 'Champion of Education, Poet, Irishmen, Patriot, Lover of Celtic Song, Author of *Father O'Flynn*'. W. H. More of Crown Lodge died in 1934. Other members of the pre-war ascendancy had earlier quit the scene. The depression deepened and it was truly 'Goodbye To All That', to quote A. P. Grave's son Robert (1895-1986), who had held the rank of captain in the R.W.F. When a pupil at Charterhouse, Robert Graves introduced the future novelist Richard Hughes (1900-1976) to this district and, much later, the author of *High Wind in Jamaica* and *In Hazard* was to make his home at Môr Edryn, on the Dwyryd estuary to the north of the town. Here he embarked on his unfinished grand novel of which he published *Fox in the Attic* and *The Wooden Shepherdess* (1973).

In 1922 the St David's Hotel was gutted by fire. It was rebuilt, but not to Walton's original design, and this provided work for many unemployed men. A few years later, John Ivor Jones (1873-1959), a son of Daniel Jones of Gwyndy Stores, opened Plas Stores and the adjoining Plas Café (the former Blue Lion). The stores catered especially for Harlech's wealthier residents and summer visitors, for they offered chocolate-coated ants and bumblebees in syrup, along with choice hams, quality cheeses and so on. It was a distinctly superior emporium. There were at least two events of some note at Harlech in 1927. Morfa Harlech was inundated by an exceptionally high tide ('Y Llanw Mawr') but fortunately no human lives were lost. In the autumn of 1927, the vacant Plas Wernfawr was purchased for around £8,000 by Henry Gethin Lewis, to serve as a college for adult students, 'Coleg Harlech'. This scheme was inspired by Dr Thomas Jones CH, Assistant Secretary to the Cabinet under Lloyd George and later prime ministers. The first Warden was Ben (later Sir Ben) Bowen Thomas. Before George Davison quit Harlech for his 'Chateau des Enfants' in the South of France, he had been instrumental in introducing the distinguished American (Bostonian) photographer Alvin Langdon Coburn (1882-1966) to this area. Coburn lived for several years at Harlech (Cae Besi) and was persuaded by the town's chemist, Daniel H. Parry (1878-1928) MPS of Cemlyn, to provide a number of local 'views' for publication. This booklet is now a collector's item.

In short, the inter-war years at Harlech were a mixture of deepening depression and more heartening moments. Many inhabitants have happy memories of this period when they were 'Brain Harlech' (Harlech Crows as they were called by their neighbouring rivals).

The Second World War added eleven more names to Harlech's War Memorial. Morfa Harlech was used as a gunnery range, and Morfa Dyffryn was converted to an airfield for fighters to intercept bombing raids on Liverpool and other cities. Evacuees from Merseyside came to the town and district, where most became fluent Welsh-speakers. Harlech beach was studded with wooden posts to prevent airborne landings, and the local Home Guard provided some reassurance spiced with touches of unintended humour in troubled times. Children played in the twelve-acre hugeness of Bronygraig, which had formerly contained Harlech's Mineral Water Works.

Post-war austerity and reconstruction were followed by a dramatic expansion of the tourist trade, as the era of motorised tourism began in earnest. Since then the small town has become much less close as a community, and its Welshness is now in serious danger, in spite of continuing efforts to halt and reverse the decline of the language. Materially, the inhabitants are distinctly better off in spite of the current recession. Colege Harlech, now in its 60th year as a residential college for adults, possesses a well equipped theatre, 'Theatr Ardudwy', in place of the former Great Hall which was sadly destroyed by fire in 1968. The district's secondary school, 'Ysgol Ardudwy', was opened in 1957 and, more recently, the primary school was moved from Rock Terrace to the foot of the castle rock ('Ysgol Tan-y-Castell'). Council and private housing estates have been developed on the Morfa below the old town. For visitors and tourists (a distinction which is now commonly ignored) the chief attractions remain the Castle, visited by well over 100,000 people each year; the Rhinogs, with their upland valleys, lakes and black streams and, of course, the fine and extensive sand beach and excellent golf course. Work remains scarce, and future prospects are clouded, but the magnificent views from Harlech's airy and rocky platform can even, at times, dispel a Welsh despondency.

Harlech Beach and Snowdonia from Frondeg, c1920. (GAS)

- CYLCHWYL GERDDOROL -

CASTELL HARLECH,

(SEFYDLWYD 1867.)

Mehefin 30ain, 1921.

CADEIRYDD Y PWYLLGOR:

MR. JOHN GRIFFITH, B.Sc., Dolgelley.

IS-GADEIRYDD:

MR. WILLIAM JONES, Pwllheli.

TRYSORYDD:

MR. H. ARIANDER HUGHES, Llanberis.

YSGRIFENYDD:

MR. W. MORRIS JONES, Portmadoc.

Yn yr Hwyr perfformir

"ST. PAUL,"

(Mendelssohn).

Argraffwyd gan Lloyd & Son, Porthmadog.

PRIS 4c.

ABOVE: Wil Jones, Pantmawr, with a pony and trap and visitors near the beach, c1920. (BEE) LEFT: Dr Thomas Jones CH, founder of Coleg Harlech, from a lithograph by Sir William Rothenstein, 1923. RIGHT: Harlech Music Festival Programme, 1921.

THE

FINEST MUSICAL TREAT IN WALES.

HARLECH CASTLE

Musical Festival

Thursday, June 23rd, 1927, at 10, 2 & 6

'MOUNT OF OLIVES' (Beethoven) | 'STABAT MATER' (Rossini)

FIFTEEN CHOIRS 1,500 VOICES

FULL ORCHESTRA—leader Mr. Akeroyd

Presidents—J. M. HOWELL, Esq. and F. C. MINOPRIO, Esq.

Conductor—DR. HOPKIN EVANS.

Artistes—

Miss Mair Jones. Miss Blodwen Hughes.
Mr. Walter Glynne. Owen Bryngwyn

Miss NELLIE ROBERTS and Miss MAY ROWLANDS.

Accompanists—Madame DAVIES HUMPHREYS, A.R.C.M., & Mr. TOM JENKINS, Mus.B.

Morning and Afternoon—Hymn Tunes and Choruses by the United Choirs, Selections by Single Choirs, Solos, and Orchestral Works.

Evening—"MOUNT OF OLIVES" and "STABAT MATER" Massed Choirs and Orchestra.

Admission (including tax) DAY Reserved Seats £1 2s. 6d.; Second 12s.; Un-reserved 8s. 6d. Reserved Seats for any Single Meeting 8s. 6d.
MORNING or AFTERNOON, First 4s. 3d.; Second 3s.; Third 1s. 10d.
EVENING, First 5s. 9d.; Second 3s. 6d.; Third 2s. 4d.
Early Bookings for Reserved Seats earnestly requested. Hymn Tunes and Words, 4d.; Mount of Olives, 6d. O.N. 1s.; Stabat Mater, 1s. O.N. 1s. 6d.; Programme and Book of Words, 4d.

Apply to W. MORRIS JONES, Portmadoc, Hon. Sec.

Cheap Bookings and Special Trains and Buses from all parts, see Bills.

16 Edward Williams, Printer, Dolgelley

THE HARLECH HISTORICAL PAGEANT.

Authors: ERNEST RHYS and ALFRED PERCEVAL GRAVES.
Musical Composer: MR. CHARLES [illegible] CLEMEN[illegible]S.
Musical Director: DR. W[illegible]LFOR[illegible] DA[illegible].
Pageant Master: MR. [illegible]ATRICK J. [illegible].

The Pageant will be presented at HARLECH throughout the Week, AUGUST 23rd-28th, in these Eight Episodes. 1922

I. THE GREAT SEA FLOOD.
Chief Characters: Prince Longshanks, Princess Eilon, The Sea Walls Keeper.

II. THE WOOING OF BRANWEN.
Chief Characters: King Bran of Britain, Matholwch, Princess Branwen.

III. OWAIN GLYNDWR'S HARLECH PARLIAMENT.
Chief Characters: Owain and Lady Glyndwr, Bishop Trevor, Chancellor Yonge. Acted chiefly by Mr. Lloyd George's Family.

IV. QUEEN MARGARET AT HARLECH CASTLE.
Chief Characters: Jasper Tudor, Edward, Prince of Wales, Queen Margaret. Acted by Lord and Lady Howard de Walden and Friends.

V. THE SEVEN YEARS DEFENCE of the CASTLE.
Chief Characters: Dafydd ap Einion and his Brothers and Cousins. Acted by Mr. Tom Ellis and Friends.

VI. ARCHDEACON PRYS AS PSALMODIST.
Chief Characters: The Archdeacon and his Lay Clerk. Acted by descendants of Archdeacon Prys.

VII. THE ROYALISTS DEFEND HARLECH.
Chief Characters: Colonel Owen and Sir Arthur Blayney, Royalists; General Mytton and Colonel Jones, Cromwellians; and Mari of the Morfa.

VIII. THE COMING OF PEACE.
Chief Characters: Old Time (Hen Amser), War (Rhyfel), Peace (Hedd). Acted by Miss Ruth Leng and Friends.

LEFT: Harlech Music Festival Poster, 1927. RIGHT: The Harlech Historical Pageant Programme, 1922. BELOW: Mediaeval costumes in the Pageant of 1922. (JH/GAS)

HARLECH MERIONETHSHIRE

DENMAN'S GWYNVA CAFE

HARLECH, Merionethshire.

Best Makes of Chocolates, Sweets, Minerals, Cigarettes, Tobaccos, &c.

LUNCHEONS AND AFTERNOON TEAS.

ICES A SPECIALITY. CIRCULATING LIBRARY and STATIONERY.

CHAR-A-BANC PARTIES CATERED FOR.

ABOVE: Spectators of the Pageant in 1922. (JH/GAS) BELOW: An advertisement from the *Wales Trade Directory*, 1927. (GAS)

King Line vessels commanded by Capt Frank Ellis in the inter-war years.
ABOVE: *King David*, CENTRE: *King James* and BELOW: *King Edgar*.

BEN ROWLANDS, MOTOR ENGINEER,

Druid Cycle and Motor Depot,

Llanfair, HARLECH, Merionethshire.

Any Make of Car and Motor Cycle Supplied.

REPAIRS FOR MOTORS AND CYCLES A SPECIALITY.

Vulcanising & all Motor & Cycle Accessories always in Stock. Tyre Stockist.

Telegrams: "Rowlands, Harlech." Tel. No. Harlech, 30.

ABOVE: Llanfair village near Harlech; the old smithy with Ben Rowlands and his nephew Dan Rowlands, c1927. BELOW: Advert from the *Wales Trade Directory* 1927, the diversification of a local trade. (GAS)

ABOVE: A group of local people outside Baptist 'Capel Bach' in Llanfair, c1930. BELOW: Llanfair looking northwards (towards Harlech), 1940s.

OPPOSITE ABOVE: Tŷ'n Llan, formerly the Crown Inn, Llanfair. Note the mounting block on the adjoining stable, c1920. (NLW) BELOW: Llanfair looking southwards with the village Post Office and shop. LEFT: 'Roman Steps', Cwm Bychan, c1920, from a photograph by A. L. Coburn. These well-made steps in wild country continue to defy explanation. RIGHT: Penllech, 1986 with Caereinion, formerly Ysgoldy (schoolhouse), and, below, Tŷ'r Felin, the mill or miller's house. (MW) BELOW: The Castle c1920, from a photograph by A. L. Coburn. (CH)

LEFT: The Williams family of Bodlondeb, Harlech, c1915. (EW)
RIGHT: *Y Ddau Frenin* (The Two Kings), commissioned by the Welsh Arts Council and sculpted by Ivor Roberts-Jones RA, 1984, 1986. (MW)
BELOW: Plas Wernfawr, c1920, from a photograph by A. L. Coburn. (CH)

ABOVE: Harlech from the air by Aerofilms Ltd. (GAS) BELOW: Ty'n-y-Groes corner looking towards Tryfer Terrace, 1986. Four-horse coaches had to negotiate this corner in either direction in the last century. (MW)

ABOVE: Pentre'r Efail looking towards Clogwyn in 1920. From a photograph by A. L. Coburn. (GAS) BELOW: Walled fields to the north of Llanfair near Harlech, c1930.

ABOVE: Some Llanfair Baptists near 'Capel Bach', c1930. (MPH)
LEFT: Llandanwg church and lych gate embedded partly in sand.
RIGHT: A wooden water wheel at Gerddi Bluog, Llanfair parish. (NLW)

ABOVE: Harlech Golf Links, c1918. (GAS) BELOW: Thomas Hughes in conversation outside Môr Anedd, c1920. (CH)

ABOVE: The Castle, Morfa Harlech and the back of Bronwen Terrace from Pen-y-Graig, c1930. (GAS) BELOW: Weighing a pig at the back of Ty'n Llan, Llanfair, c1930. David Williams, Ty'n Llan (right), and John Pugh. (JW)

ABOVE: Plas Café (formerly the Blue Lion Inn) and verandah, c1930. (MR) BELOW: Plas Stores and Café, c1930, when John Ivor Jones (formerly of Gwyndy Stores) was proprietor. The Stores, a superior emporium, were opened in 1926-7. (MR)

ABOVE: The interior of Plas Café, c1930. This had been the dining room of the former Blue Lion Inn opened in about 1830. (MR) BELOW: Harlech from the north: Tanllech, Llech and Penllech, c1930. (CH)

Coleg Harlech, c1940. (CH)

ABOVE: The workshop at Coleg Harlech, c1950. (CH) BELOW: The Great Hall, Coleg Harlech, c1960.

LEFT: Coleg Harlech Library from below, c1960. (CH) RIGHT: Theatr Ardudwy from the courtyard of Coleg Harlech, c1975. (CH)

The Castle and its steep backdrop from the air by Aerofilms Ltd. (GAS)

Bibliography

Manuscript Sources

Most relevant materials are in the Public Record Office (PRO), the National Library of Wales (NLW), Aberystwyth, the Archives of the University College of North Wales, Bangor, and the Gwynedd Archives at Caernarfon and Dolgellau. The sources quoted in the mediaeval and early modern sections of the text have been drawn principally from transcriptions made by W. W. E. Wynne of Peniarth and published in *Archaeologia Cambrensis (Arch. Camb.)* as listed in the Index to *Arch.Camb.* 1846-1900 under 'Harlech'. Other materials cited are conveniently catalogued in the above centres.

Official Reports, Newspapers and Trade Directories.

Two official reports have been cited: *Reports of the Charity Commissioners (Wales)* (1836) and the *Report of the Commission of Inquiry into the State of Education in Wales, Part III (North Wales)* (1847). Just two weekly newspapers have been consulted closely and cited: the *Carnarvon Herald* (1831-36) and the *Carnarvon and Denbigh Herald* (from 1836). Various trade directories have been examined from the 1820s onwards including *Pigot, Pigot and Slater* and *Slater's Directories (North and South Wales).*

Printed Books and Articles.

This selective list includes some books and articles in Welsh.

Allan, Ian George Walton at Harlech *Journal of the Merioneth Historical and Record Society (JMH&RS)* X 71-84

Baker, Dennis, An Eighteenth Century Drover: William (Rowlands) of Tan-y-Bwlch *JMH&RS* VI 372-380

Bingley, Rev W. *Excursions in North Wales* (3rd Edn. 1839)

Bowen, E. G. Merioneth in the Dark Ages *JMH&RS* II 169-177; *Saints Seaways and Settlements in Celtic Lands* (1969)

Bowen, E. G. and Gresham, C. *The History of Merioneth* Vol. I (1967)

Bradley, A. G. *In Praise of North Wales* (1925)

Camden's *Britannia* (1695)

Cecil-Williams, J. L. C. Obituary to Sir Vincent Evans (1852-1934) *Transactions of the Honourable Society of Cymmrodorion (THSC)* (1936) 183-188

Davies, David ('Dewi Eden') *Ardudwy a'i Gwron* (1914)

Davies, Elwyn, Hendre and Hafod in Merioneth *JMH&RS* VII 13-27

Davies, V. Challinor, Some Geographical Aspects of the Decline in the Rural Population of Wales with Special Reference to Merioneth *JMH&RS* II, 58-65

Davies, Walter *General View of the Agriculture of Wales* (1810)

Davies, W. Ll., Phylipiaid Ardudwy — A Survey and a Summary *Y Cymmrodor* XLII 155-268

Dempster Jones, Tom, Happy was I in Harlech town *Country Quest* Vol. 15 No. 1 (June 1974) 24-25 (An extract from the author-artist's book *Another Span of Life*)

Dodd, A. H. *The Industrial Revolution in North Wales* (3rd Edn. 1971)

Eames, A., Lloyd, L. and Parry, B. *Letters From America* (1975)

Eckley, Martin and Lloyd, Lewis *Cwmwd Ardudwy* (1985)

Edwards, Fanny, *Penrhyndeudraeth, JMH&RS* I 197-201

Evans, D. L., Walter de Manny, Sheriff of Merioneth, *JMH&RS* IV 194-203

Evans, Rev J. *Letters written during a Tour Through North Wales* (3rd Edn. 1804); *A Topographical and Historical Description of North Wales* (1810)

Evans, Ven. A. Owen, Edmund Prys: Archdeacon of Merioneth, Priest, Preacher, Poet (1544-1623) *THSC* (1924) 112-161.

Fenton, Richard *A Tour in Quest of Genealogy* (1811); *Tours in Wales (1804-1813)* (1917)

Godwin, Fay and Toulson, Shirley *The Drovers Roads of Wales* (1977)

Graves, Robert von Ranke *Goodbye To All That* (1929)

Gresham, C. A. and Hemp, W. J. Lasynys *JMH&RS* III 79-84

Gresham, Colin, The Harlech Pageant, 1922 *JMH&RS* IX 97-105; Nanmor Deudraeth, *JMH&RS* VIII 97-121

Gwynedd Jones, Ieuan, Merioneth Politics in Mid-Nineteenth Century: The Politics of a Rural Economy *JMH&RS* V 273-334
Howell, David W. Merioneth Agriculture and the Farming Community a century ago *JMH&RS* VIII 71-96
Hucks, J. *A Pedestrian Tour Through North Wales* (1795)
Hughes, Emrys and Eames, Aled *Porthmadog Ships* (1975)
Hughes, Harold, Harlech Castle *Arch.Camb.* XIII (1913) 275-316
Hughes, Henry *Immortal Sails* (2nd Edn. 1969)
Jarrett, Michael G. Excavations at Tomen-y-Mur *JMH&RS* IV 171-175
Jeffreys Jones, T. I., The Pumrhydau and Corsydd of the Parish of Llandanwg *JMH&RS* II 143-148
Jeffreys Jones, T. I. Dyddiadur Robert Jones, Cefnfilltir *JMH&RS* III 318-322
Jenkins, J. Geraint *The Welsh Woollen Industry* (1969); Rural Industry in Merioneth *JMH&RS* VIII 1-15
Jones, E. D. Robert Vaughan of Hengwrt *JMH&RS* I 21-30; Camden, Vaughan, and Llwyd, and Merionethshire *JMH&RS* II 209-227
Jones, E. Rosalie *A History of Barmouth and its Vicinity* (1909)
Jones, Emyr Gwynne, Manuscripts Relating to Merioneth at Bangor, 1. — The Maesyneuadd Collection *JMH&RS* III 184-192
Jones, Emyr Wyn, The Quest for a Crown *JMH&RS* X 1-28 (Barmouth's significance in the Lancastrian/Tudor cause, 1468-1485, is discussed)
Jones, J. Gordon The Ffestiniog Slate Industry: The Industrial Pattern to 1831 *JMH&RS* VI 50-65; The Ffestiniog Slate Industry: The Industrial Pattern, 1831-1913 *JMH&RS* VI 191-213
Jones, M. J. The Merioneth Woollen Industry, 1758-1820 *Y Cymmrodor* (1939)
Jones, R. Merfyn *The North Wales Quarrymen, 1874-1922* (1981) Studies in Welsh History 4
Jones, Thomas Iorwerth, The Contribution of Welshmen to Science *THSC* (1934) 40-232, at 214-216 regarding Dr John Thomas (1886-1932) of Harlech as a leading industrial chemist
Jones Pierce, T. *Mediaeval Welsh Society* (1972) — selected essays edited by J. Beverley Smith
Jones-Roberts, K. W. and Davies, Sir W. Ll. Pengwern, Ffestiniog *JMH&RS* I 180-184
Jones-Roberts, K. W. Historic Houses in Ffestiniog and District *JMH&RS* III 263-274
Lewis, E. A. *Mediaeval Boroughs of Snowdonia* (1929)
Lindsay, Jean *A History of the North Wales Slate Industry* (1974)
Lloyd, John Ellis Wynne o Las Ynys *JMH&RS* I 31-68; Llanfair Juxta Harlech *JMH&RS* II 89-94; Colonel John Jones, Maesygarnedd *JMH&RS* II 95-104; Llanbedr ar Artro *JMH&RS* II 197-203; The Will of Dr John Ellis of Dolgelley (1647, 1665) *JMH&RS* II 228-231
Lloyd, John Llanfihangel y Traethau *JMH&RS* III 137-150
Lloyd, Lewis W. The Ivorites of Harlech *JMH&RS* VI 372-380; *The Town and Port of Barmouth, 1565-1973* (1974); *The Unity of Barmouth* (1977); *The Ship Aground* (1977); Some Ardudwy Cattle Drovers *JMH&RS* VII 118-120; The Last Lloyd of Cwm Bychan: John Lloyd (1826-1911) of Bala, Kansas — An Essay in Family Reconstruction *JMH&RS* VII 251-282 and 431-2; Captain William Lewis (1833-1882) *Cymru a'r Môr/Maritime Wales (MW)* 1(1976)126-7; The Schooner *Factor* of Barmouth and her Voyage to West Africa in 1836 *MW* 2(1977)19-27; Llanfair Slate Quarry *Bulletin of the Gwynedd Archives Service (BGAS)* (there is also a Welsh edition) 2(1975) 24-30; Travelling Men: Drovers and Mariners and the Evidence of Three Letters *BGAS* 3(1976) 28-42; and Eckley, Martin *Hen Dref Harlech a Phentre Llanfair* (1978); Harlech and Ardudwy, 1880-1930 *JMH&RS* VIII 16-26; The Note Book of James Anwyl of Harlech *MW* 3 (1978) 53-56; Corsygedol, Ardudwy's Principal Estate *JMH&RS* VIII 27-60 and 157-190; Capt. Lewis Holland-Thomas of Caerffynnon Hall, Talsarnau *MW* 4 (1979) 89-95;The Wreck of the Ship *Lancaster* on Sarn Badrig *MW* 4 (1979) 116-117; Brigs, Snows and Brigantines: Mawddach Square-riggers to 1827 *JMH&RS* VIII 237-276, 369-396 and IX 17-66, 179-223 and 308-324; Captain Frank Ellis (1876-1971): A Seaman of Harlech *MW* — 8 (1984) 100-127; The Nightmare Voyage to New York of the Emigrant Ship *Oregon* in 1849 *MW* 7 (1983) 118-120
Lloyd-Hughes, D. G. David Williams, Castell Deudraeth, and the Merioneth Elections, 1859, 1865 and 1868 *JMH&RS* V 335-349
Lord Harlech Glyn Cywarch *JMH&RS* I 9-11
Morgan, Richard Robert Vaughan of Hengwrt (? 1592-1667) *JMH&RS* VIII 397-408
Nicholas, Sir Harry (Ed.) *Proceedings and Ordinances of the Privy Council of England* (1834)
Owen, Heulwen and Hedydd Isambard *The Caerffynnon Story* (1973)
Owen, Hugh J. *Merioneth Volunteers and Local Militia* (1934); *Echoes of Old Merioneth* (1944); *Treasures of the Mawddach* (1950); *From Merioneth to Botany Bay* (1952); Owen Glyndŵr's Old Parliament House at Dolgelley *JMH&RS* II 81-88
Owen, R. *Hanes Methodistiaeth Gorllewin Meirionnydd* (1891)

Parry, Henry *Wreck and Rescue on the Coast of Wales* Vol. I (The Life Boats of Cardigan Bay and Anglesey) (1969)
Peers, C. R. Harlech Castle *THSC* (1923) 63-82
Pevsner, Nikolaus George Walton His Life and Work *Journal of the Royal Institute of British Architects* (3 April 1939) 537-548
Price, R. Emyr Lloyd George and Merioneth Politics, 1885, 1886 — a failure to effect a breakthrough *JMH&RS* VII 292-307. In 1886 the Harlech Liberals favoured David Lloyd George as candidate but the county adopted Thomas Edward Ellis who was M.P. from 1886 until his death in 1899.
Pritchard, R. T. Merionethshire Roads and Turnpike Trusts *JMH&RS* IV 22-36
Rees, D. Morgan Industrial Archaeology in Merioneth *JMH&RS* V 133-146; *Industrial Archaeology of Wales* (1975)
Richards, Melville The Marriage Settlement of Ellen, Daughter of Ellis Wynne of Lasynys, 1724 *JMH&RS* III 296-301
Roberts, Peter R. The Social History of the Merioneth Gentry *circa* 1660-1840 *JMH&RS* IV 216-229; The Merioneth Gentry and Local Government *circa* 1650-1838 *JMH&RS* V 21-38.
Roscoe, Thomas *Wanderings and Excursions in North Wales* (1836)
Smith, Peter *Houses in the Welsh Countryside* (1975); Corsygedol *JMH&RS* II 285-291
Souslby, Ian *The Mediaeval Towns of Wales* (1983). Brief and rather misleading as to Harlech at pp. 138-9.
Stead, Peter *Coleg Harlech* (1977)
Stephenson, David, Dr. *The Last Prince of Wales 1282-1283* (1982)
Taylor, A. J. *The King's Works in Wales, 1277-1330* (HMSO London 1974). Reprinted from *The History of the King's Works*, edited by H. M. Colvin (HMSO 1963).
Thomas, Ben Bowen (Ed.) *Harlech Studies* (1938). N. B. Robert Richards' Ardudwy and its Ancient Churches 165-204 and R. Glyn Lloyd's Eglwysi Ardudwy 205-213
Thomas, Colin Merioneth Estates, 1790-1850: A Study in Agrarian Geography *JMH&RS* V 221-238; The Corsygedol Estate During 'The Age of Improvement' *JMH&RS* VI 303-310; Patterns and Processes of Estate Expansion in the Fifteenth and Sixteenth Centuries *JMH&RS* VI 333-342; Livestock Numbers in Mediaeval Gwynedd *JMH&RS* VII 113-117
Thomas, Gwyn Ellis Wynne of Lasynys *JMH&RS* VI 137-147
Thomas, Peter D. G. The Parliamentary Representation of Merioneth During the Eighteenth Century *JMH&RS* III 128-136
Tucker, Norman *North Wales in the Civil War* (1958); *Royalist Officers of North Wales 1642-1660* (1961); The Last Flag Comes Down *JMH&RS* IV 16-21; The Civil War in Merioneth *JMH&RS* IV 212-215
Vaughan, Mary Nannau *JMH&RS* IV 119-121 and 204-207
Whitney, Catherine Notes Concerning Gypsies with Special Reference to Abram Wood *JMH&RS* VI 359-367
Williams, David *A History of Modern Wales* (2nd Edn. 1977)
Wright, G. N. *Scenes in North Wales* (1833)
Wynne Jones, Ivor *Shipwrecks of North Wales* (1973) 23-38 (Cardigan Bay)

Harlech Hunt and Races.

For many years past this meeting had been annually held at Harlech, but through some unfortunate circumstances, it did not take place in 1850. This year, by the exertions of the young men of the neighbourhood, it was held as usual on Tuesday and Wednesday, the 21st and 22nd ult., and we are happy to say, the successful termination of the meeting surpassed the most sanguine expectations of its promoters.

On Tuesday, Mr. Jones, of Ynysfawr's celebrated hounds met on the Glyn marsh. The field was numerous and respectable, and the sport decidedly excellent. There were four splendid runs, traversing the whole of the flat land under Harlech, and puss was taken and saved in each run.

At four o'clock all returned to Harlech to partake of a most exeellent dinner, prepared by the worthy landlady, Mrs. Foulkes, in that style, for which she is proverbial, John Walker, Esq., Hendregadredd, presided, and Griffith Jones Williams, Esq., Dolgelley, officiated as vice.

After the cloth had been removed, and the usual loyal toasts proposed, and cordially responded to,

The Chairman proposed the health of the "Lord Lieutenant," and the "Member for the County."

In proposing "Prosperity to all future hunts at Harlech," the Chairman hoped this was only the commencement of a series of similar excellent meetings; and remarked upon the benefit of making reasonable charges at such meetings. He was glad to find that the landlady in the present instance had attended strictly to this rule, thereby enabling many respectable parties to join the meeting, who otherwise could not have attended (*the toast was drunk with three times three*).

The Chairman next called upon the company to drink to the memory of "Col. Vaughan, the first patron of Harleoh Hunt," which was done accordingly in solemn silence.

By the Vice—The health of "Sir Robert Vaughan." No one regretted the downfall of the old Harlech Hunt more than he, and he (the speaker) felt confident that when Sir Robert was informed of its revival, he would liberally support its future meetings (*drunk with three times three*).

By the Chair—The health of "Mr. G. J. Williams," an active member of the old hunt, and one who had always used his utmost endeavours to maintain it. Now it had gone, he came forward with right good will to give his valuable services in behalf of the new one.

Mr. Williams returned thanks, and called upon Mr. Matron Williams for a song.

Mr. Williams sang "The Lass that loves a Sailor," to the great delight of the company.

The 'Sport of Kings'.

Index

ABOVE: Modernity: Coleg Harlech's new residential tower block from the Golf Links, c1968. (CH)

Subscribers

Presentation Copies

1 Meirionnydd Council
2 Harlech Community Council
3 Gwynedd Library Services
4 Gwynedd Archives
5 Coleg Harlech
6 Jim Yuill

7 Lewis Lloyd
8 Clive & Carolyn Birch
9 R.B. Conway
10 M.J. Bryant
11 W.R. Holton
12
13 F.W. Smith
14 Mr & Mrs E. Henderson
15 Hilary Lewis
16 R.W. Burgin
17 Lawrence Lamb
18 Huw Davies
19 Peter G. Jones
20
21 Ann Smith
22
25 Paul Rogers
26 Ken Birch
27 Dr E.D. Jones
28 Dennis Webb
29 J.P. Williams Jones
30 Mrs Megan Reeves
31 Stuart Ian Gregory
32
33 Rufus Adams
34 Anton Bantock
35 Peter Lloyd Beale
36 Allen Geoffrey Lloyd Beale
37 Dr L.J. & Mrs MacFarlane
38 Alun A. Nelson
39 Victoria & Albert Museum
40 London Guildhall Library
41 James Anwyl-Nelson
42 Hâf Williams
43 Mrs Eirwen M. Williams
44 R. Gwynedd Williams
45 Peter Whitehouse
46 Clive Coles
47 G.W. Preston
48 Mrs E. Cooper
49 Mrs L. Thomas
50 Mrs N. Thomas
51 Mrs Eleanor Owen
52 Mrs Soar
53 Dewi Langley
54 Miss Mary Thomas
55 Miss Bronwen Thomas
56 Gordon & Stella Calvert
57 Glyn Roberts
58 Ieuan Gwynedd Jones
59 Margaret Kendall
60
61 Miss A. Jones
62 N. Jeffreys-Jones
63 Barry Moore
64 G. Hitchcock
65 Brynmor Thomas
66 P.J. Twamley
67 Timothy Dowding
68 Mrs A. Edwards
69 Gladys Jones Sharp
70 S.J.F. O'Connell
71 Mrs G.A. Davies
72 T. Williams
73 Fred Foskett
74 Charles H. Gorton
75 Mrs M.L. Gorton
76 Cecelia Biesty
77 Dr J. Crowe
78 Clive Coles
79 Heather Evans
80 G. Griffith
81
88 Jim & Betty Yuill
89 Joan Allen
90 Gill & Jim Kelsey
91 Willem & Barbara Alting von Geusau
92 Betty Ayling
93 Mathew Allen
94 Dilys & Gordon Brown
95 Rob J. Hall
96 Chas & Maureen Wing
97 Mr & Mrs Slatter
98 Mrs & Mrs Horsefield
99 Mr & Mrs I.W. Rowlands
100 R.M. Thomas
101 G. Evans
102 J.M. Bamford
103 Mrs N. Halewood
104 J.B. Mills
105 Ken Brown
106 L.R. Oliver
107 N. Brown
108 D. Lumb
109 Hugh Davies
110 Terence Jackson
111 R.E. Roberts
112 Simon Proctor
113 T.A. Richards
114 Geoff & Eirwen
115 David Gareth Evans
116 Frederick Foskett
117 Michael James Meller
118 Miss Lowri W. Jones
119 Miss Megan Griffiths
120 John Shaw
121 Nicholas Hopkins
122 Dafydd Williams
123 Phillip Blériot Williams
124 W.E. Parry
125 Mrs M.W. Parry
126 Malcolm Abraham
127 K.J. Riddington
128 Sharon Trower
129 Peter Gipson
130 John Selwyn Davies
131 B.G. Freeman
132 Mrs Mair Highley
133 Brian & Jean Roberts
134 Charles Preston
135 Mrs Bessie Roberts
136 Alastair John Thompson
137 John & Jill Houliston
138 M. Farn
139 Mr & Mrs T. Tudor
140 John Smith
141 Mrs G. Parfitt
142 John Daniels
143 David Edwards Hughes
144 Jason Henry Hughes
145 Gavin Richard Hughes
146 Sian Rhisiart

147 Eve Crowe
148 David Robert John
149 Caoimhghin Mac Gearailt
150 Twm Elias
151 Peter Crew
152 Plas Tan Y Bwlch
153 Merfyn Williams
154 Alun Richards
155 Mona Williams
156 D.M. Jones
157 Alun Davies
158 G. Hughes
159 Mary, John & Rachel James
160 Eric Tutton
161 A.L.J. & G. Millar
162 Margery E. Warren
163 Dilys Ann Lloyd
164 Jean Formston
165 Peter Smith
166 Royal Commission on Ancient Monuments
167 Richard Suggett
168 Eileen Richardson
169 Cliff Barker
170 Martin J. Price
171 Michael Moule
172 Helen Haworth
173 Jane Roberts
174 Mrs Korina Mort
175
176 Mr & Mrs R. Jones
177 Mrs N. Williams
178 Mrs E. Jones
179 Mr & Mrs J. Daniels
180 A. Watson
181 John Williams
182 Eleri Price
183 Drs Tresca & Peter Winteringham
184 Joan Smith
185 Ian Smith
186 Richard Evans
187 Augusto Gatta
188 Iwan Morris
189 Marion Roberts
190 John Lewis
191 John Artro Morris
192 Allen Lamey & Family
193 Merfyn & Blodwen Hughes
194 Rhys Rhisiart
195 Mrs V. Hughes
196 Mrs B. Murphy
197 The University College of Wales
198 Mrs Ellen Oakley
199 Alan Morris
200
202 Lewis Lloyd
203 Michael Evans
204 Margaret A. Jones
205 Miss Mair E. Edwards
206 Jon Parry
207 Rob Turner
208 Betty & Glen Jones
209 Mr & Mrs P.J. Williams
210 Elisabeth & Neil Evans
211 Martin Eckley
212 Llyfrgell Coleg Harlech
213 Edgar Parry Williams
214 Llyfrgell Coleg
215 Harlech
216 Silyn Hughes
217 Terence Penny
218 Merfyn a Linda Tomos
219 Gwynfa Adam
220 Mena Ifans
221 David & Patricia Henderson
222 Valmai Owen
223 Marian Jones
224 Richard Poole
225 Peter Thompson
226 Philip Morris
227 J.E.F. Lauder
228 Wendon Wigglesworth
229 Eluned Roberts
230 R.W. Benn
231 A.B. John
232 Mrs Esther Owen
233 Mrs Morfudd Thomas
234 Wil John
235 Louise Thomas
236 Mrs Margaret Beale
237 Mrs R.M.D. Lloyd
238 Mrs W.I.B. Shaw
239 Richard Powell Williams
240 Angharad Jones
241 John A. Ebbs
242 D.R. John
243 R. Griffiths
244 Enid M. Jones
245 James John Shewring
246 Ernest Mark Scriven
247 George Vincent Jones
248
249 Mrs Mair M. Williams
250 Quentin Cartwright
251 Karen Lyle
252 Phil Mostert
253 Gwyndaf Huws
254 Ian Osborne Roberts
255 D.A. Pestell
256 A. McNally
257 Humphrey Williams
258 Trevor V. Jones
259 H. Eilir Owen
260 Miss Mair Lloyd
261 Arwel Jones
262 John C. Fairweather
263 Ellen F. Clark
264 Jacqueline White
265 Barbara J. Garrett
266 John C. Fairweather
267 Mr & Mrs E.C. Lloyd
268 Aled & Freda Eames
269 Gordon & Stella Calvert
270 Mrs Ann E. Jones
271 Mrs Gwyneth Lloyd Ruffell
272 Meurig R. Jones
273 Glyn Williams
274 Graham Biswell
275 Bob Major
276 R.K. Griffiths
277 E. Ainsworth
278 Brian Ashton
279 Dave Robinson
280 Mrs Bethan Jones
281 Mrs E. Parsons
282 Mrs M. Pierce
283
284 J.K. Goody
285 Douglas Owen
286 Colin A. Cornish

Remaining names unlisted.

ENDPAPERS: Ardudwy from John Speede's map of Merioneth, 1610. (CH)

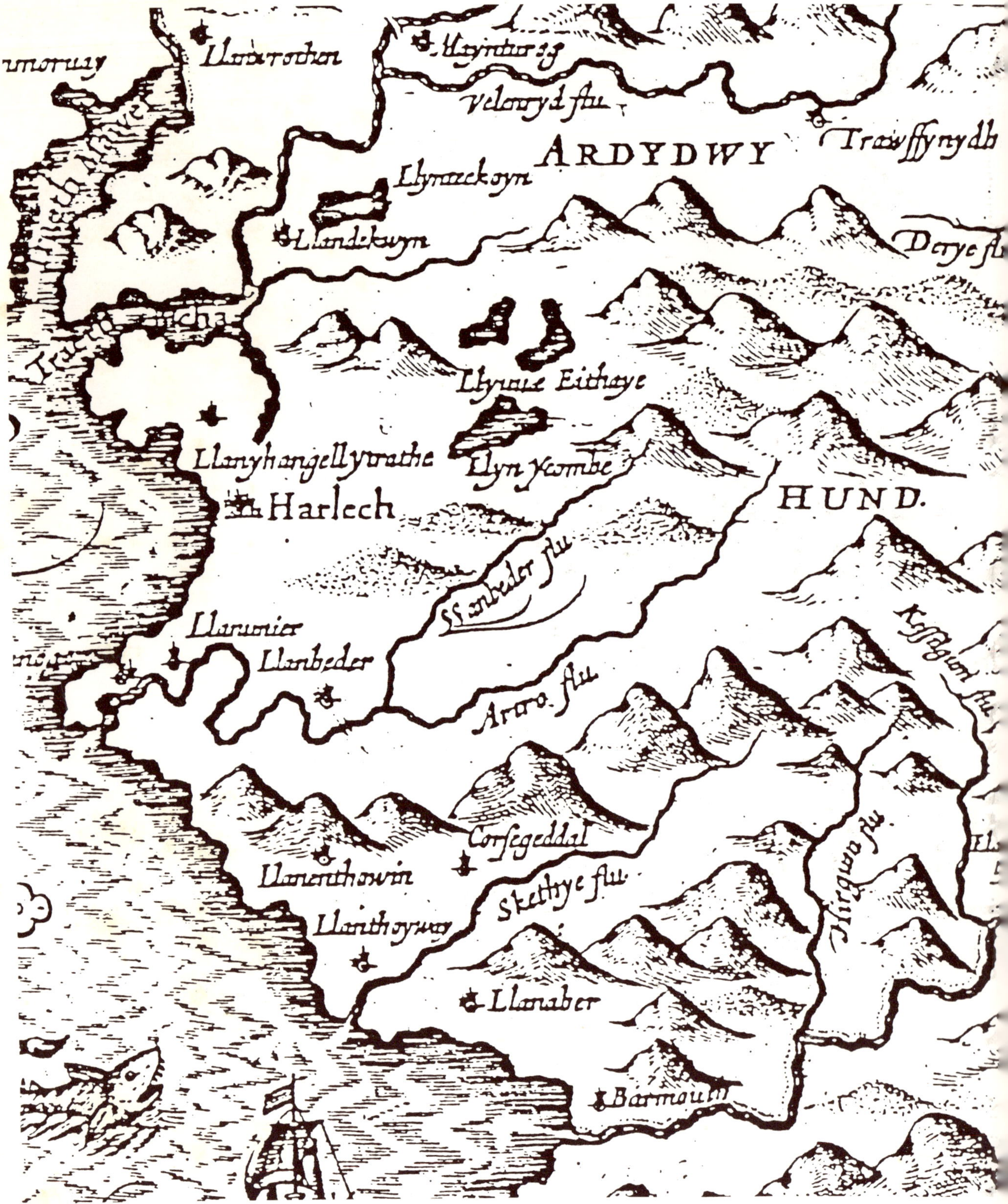
ARDYDWY
HUND.
Harlech
Llanbeder
Llanaber
Barmouth